D0201300

14.40

THINKING
ABOUT GOD

FIRST STEPS
IN PHILOSOPHY

GREGORY E. GANSSLE

InterVarsity Press
Downers Grove, Illinois

InterVarsity Press
P.O. Box 1400, Downers Grove, IL 60515-1426
World Wide Web: www.ivpress.com
E-mail: mail@ivpress.com

InterVarsity Press® is the book-publishing division of InterVarsity Christian Fellowship/USA®, a student movement active on campus at hundreds of universities, colleges and schools of nursing in the United States of America, and a member movement of the International Fellowship of Evangelical Students. For information about local and regional activities, write Public Relations Dept., InterVarsity Christian Fellowship/USA, 6400 Schroeder Rd., P.O. Box 7895, Madison, WI 53707-7895, or visit the IVCF website at <www.intervarsity.org>.

Design: Cindy Kiple

Images: Bill Poque/Getty Images

ISBN 0-8308-2784-6

Printed in the United States of America ∞

Library of Congress Cataloging-in-Publication Data
Ganssle, Gregory E., 1956-
  Thinking about God: first steps in philosophy / Gregory E.
Ganssle.
     p. cm.
  Includes bibliographical references and index.
  ISBN 0-8308-2784-6 (pbk.: alk paper)
  1. God 2. Christianity—Philosophy. I. Title.
  BT103.G36 2004
  211—dc22

2004017275

P	19	18	17	16	15	14	13	12	11	10	9	8	7	6	5	4	3	2	1
Y	19	18	17	16	15	14	13	12	11	10	09	08	07	06	05	04			

For David, Nicholas and Elizabeth,

who bring joy and laughter to our lives

CONTENTS

PART THREE: GOD AND EVIL

PART FOUR: WHAT IS GOD LIKE?

ACKNOWLEDGMENTS

It is a privilege to thank the many people who helped this project along. First of all, I want to thank the students in my philosophy class at Christian Heritage School. Over the past several years, they have taught me how to think more clearly in order to communicate complicated arguments in the language of actual human beings. Much of this book was field tested there. David Fullerton, in particular, has been a big help and encouragement. I have not lost hope that he will eventually switch from physics to philosophy.

InterVarsity Press provided two anonymous readers who each gave me detailed comments on the text. I am deeply indebted to them for their careful criticisms. This book is much better because of their efforts. Gary Deddo, my editor at InterVarsity Press, has been quite helpful. I am grateful to him for seeing the merit in this project, for then seeing it through to completion and, most of all, for his friendship.

I also want to thank Oxford University Press for permission to quote from *The Oxford Dictionary of Philosophy* by Simon Blackburn in chapter thirteen. Parts of chapter four come from my paper, "Copernicus, Christology and Hell: Faith Seeking Understanding," which was published in the journal *Philosophia Christi* (vol. 20, no.2 [1997]: 1-13). I thank the editor for permission to reuse some of that material.

Finally, I am delighted to thank my family. My wife, Jeanie, is always great fun. Her support, love and friendship are my greatest treasures. Nothing in my life would be what it is without her. Our children, David, Nick and Elizabeth, had to bear up under many dinner conversations about the puzzles in this book. We laughed a lot. It gives me great pleasure to dedicate this book to them.

1

WHY BOTHER THINKING ABOUT GOD?

Another book about God? Why bother? With thousands of books (and thousands of gods) on the market, why write another one? You might be thinking that since I am a philosopher, I have no life. All I can *do* after all, is think. Philosophers cannot *do* anything else. We do not do lab experiments. We have no expensive equipment. We just think. Since thinking looks like doing nothing, we try to write our thoughts down. At least if we are writing, it looks as though we are working. Usually we think about what other philosophers have thought about, and we write our thoughts down hoping still other philosophers will read them and think about our thoughts. Generally we think that our thoughts are right, and we hope to persuade fellow philosophers that we are right about being right. All the while, our fellow philosophers, who often are our friends, are doing their own thinking and writing their thoughts down and hoping to convince us that their thoughts are right. Sometimes philosophers persuade other philosophers to change their minds. Sometimes they do not.

Why bother with another book? More to the point, why bother with *this* sort of book? Let me tell you why I bother. Many philosophers have a secret dream. We think that we are good at thinking, and we dream that maybe we can help other people think better. We dream that real people—normal people—might read something we write and be better thinkers as a result. So sometimes philosophers write things with regular people in mind. Nowadays, of course, philosophers think usually about the thoughts of other philosophers and write things so only other philosophers will care to read them. It was not always this way, however. This trend is rather late in the history of philosophy. Most of the history of philosophy consists of people thinking about things and writing or discussing them in a way that allowed lots of people to take part in the conversation. I write this book because I also have this dream. I would like to help some people think better about things that they probably think about a little bit anyway. This is why I bother to write.

Just because I have a reason to write, however, does not mean that you have a reason to read. After all, you are the one who is holding this book and reading this sentence. There is a good chance that you are thinking about putting it down. You know why *I* bother to write, but why should *you* bother to keep reading? This question is a good one. Given that this is a book called *Thinking About God*, there are two parts to the question. First, why bother *thinking*? Second, why bother thinking about *God*?

Why bother thinking? Thinking is a bit unusual today. Actually it is more than unusual. It seems to be *out of style*. I suppose it is not thinking itself that is out of style, but thinking *in public* or *admitting* that you do think or need to think. Let me tell you a story that shows that I am right. If you watch a press conference on TV or one of those talk shows that discusses current issues (never mind the ones where fistfights break out), there is one thing that you will never see. You will never see a participant think. It does not matter if it is a politician answering questions, a journalist asking them or the commentators commentating on them, you will never see any of them say any sentence resembling this one: "Gee, my opponent has made a very good point, I will have to give it some careful thought."

There must be some reason that we never hear sentences of this type. I am not sure what the reason is, but I have two theories. My first theory is a bit more charitable than my second. This theory is that we do not hear people stop and think or even admit that they need to think because all of the people in the public eye have done all of their thinking already. They spent the first half of their lives thinking through all of the tough issues, and now they do not need to think anymore. They can respond instantaneously and with confidence to any conceivable question or challenge, and they never have to change their minds.

My second theory is, I am sorry to say, a bit cynical. We never hear public figures admit that they need to think because they are of the opinion that thinking shows weakness. If I have to pause to think, others will begin to get the idea that my opponent might be right, and I cannot allow that to happen. I do not mean this theory to apply only to politicians. It applies to public figures in every field. Entertainers also do not think in public. I have never seen an actor or actress, after winning some award, respond to the journalist's question about what comes next with anything like the following answer: "I am really pleased to win this award, and now I want to take some extended time to reflect on the nature and application of virtue in contemporary life."

Admitting that you think, you see, is a bit out of style. Even though thinking is out of style, there are some reasons to do it anyway. First, styles change. You never know when thinking will come back into style, and you want to be prepared. Second, you may not believe me, but all of the cool people think. If you want to be cool (and I know that you do, even if you will not admit it), then you had better think too. Now you might think that this second reason is not a very good reason. I agree. I bring it up because it leads directly into my third reason that it is worth the effort to think. The third reason is that *you cannot help it*. You *must* think. You *always* think. You *cannot refrain from* thinking. How do I know that these claims are true? You see, you are thinking *now*. I know you are thinking now because you *thought* my second reason was not very good. Therefore, you considered it and weighed it against some idea of what counts as a good reason and what does not, and you concluded that it came up short. You were thinking the whole time. I caught you. Since I caught you red-handed, you might as well admit that you think.

What is the point? If you cannot help but think, you want to think as well as possible. You want to believe things for good reasons and not for bad ones. You want to be able to evaluate reasons to see if they are good or bad. So, even though it is not popular to admit that we think, we all do it. We might as well bother enough to do it well.

Why think about *God?* After all, no one knows whether there is a God, much less which God is real. Well, I am not as sure as you that *no one* knows. If God exists, then he knows, to be sure. He would have no identity crisis. Besides, we ought not claim that no one knows that there is a God until *after* we have done our thinking about God. So one reason to bother thinking about God is to see if you can find good reasons to think that there is a God. Another reason is to see if you can find good reasons to think there is no such person as God.

There are other reasons to think about God besides trying to figure out if there is such a person. What you believe and think about God affects nearly every area of your life. Many of the big and deep questions that shape how each of us sees the world are very closely related to questions about God. For example, it is a big and important question whether life has any meaning or purpose other than whatever meaning we give it ourselves. If we push this question very far, we will wind up thinking about God. If there is a God who created us and knows us, then whatever purpose we have will probably be related to whatever purpose he has for us. Another big and important question has to do with the nature of moral reality. Are there things that are right or wrong regardless of the opinions of others? Again, if God has a purpose for us, it might be that his purpose involves our living up to or reflecting moral reality. You can see that the question of God is a central question. If we want to think well about our lives, we will want to do some of our best thinking about God.

So in this book we will think about God. We will think about what God is like, and we will think about reasons to think there is such a person as well as reasons to think there is not. I invite you to do the thinking about God and not just to let me do the thinking for you. Along the way you will find that I say things that you think are wrong. I hope that I will say other things that you think are right. Before we begin to think about God, however, we need to clear some ground so we can think well. In the next few chapters we will think about some issues that will help us see straight and think well.

2

WHAT IS PHILOSOPHY?

This book is called *Thinking About God: First Steps in Philosophy.* When we undertake to think about God, we are doing philosophy. Philosophy is the name of an academic discipline, but it is also a kind of *activity.* Now philosophy brings to many people's minds strange pictures such as that of a robed guru sitting on top of a mountain reciting deep but obscure phrases. I do not think that this picture of philosophy is very helpful. (I am not much of a mountain climber and robes make me look fat.) What is philosophy anyway, and how does a person do philosophy? Let me tell you a story that will illustrate what philosophers do.

Do you remember the TV show *Star Trek?* I know there have been several different shows of the same type. In each one, there is a starship. In nearly every episode some group of the crew meets at the transporter room and is "beamed" to the surface of a planet. They stand in the right place in this huge machine and the engineer flips the switch. Usually a tinkling noise follows along with some special effects. Then the crew disappears. The camera cuts to the surface of the planet while the same noise and effects occur and the crew materializes on the planet. They have been transported from the ship to the planet. It is quite a helpful device to have for interplanetary travel.

Well, if you take an engineer and a philosopher aboard the starship *Enterprise* and show each of them the transporter, they will ask the same question: "How does it work?" They will want to know different things, however. The engineer will want to know all about the mechanics of the machine, that is, the technology. The philosopher will want to know why we think the person who appeared on the planet and the person who was transported from the ship are one and the same.

The engineer will want to know what it is about the *machine doing the transporting* that makes the transportation possible. The philosopher will want to know what it is about the *person being transported* that allows him or her to be transported successfully. In other words, what are the conditions that must be satisfied in order to be sure that the person we call "Captain Kirk" who appears on the planet is really Captain Kirk? We all agree that it is Kirk on the planet. The philosopher wants to know what makes it Kirk. You see, if the transporter works, then *how* it works will give us some clues about what it means to be a person. Let us think together about a few possibilities.

Suppose the transporter works this way. First, it carefully takes Kirk apart while recording in great detail every step of the process. Next, the transporter takes these biological parts (let us say they are molecules) and ships them to the planet. Once they arrive on the surface, the pieces are put back together according to the strict information that was recorded. So every piece is placed in the exact position and in the exact state of motion it was in before Kirk was dissolved. In this system, the transporter beams both information and material. We can call this the "information-and-guts method." If this is how the transporter works, we might be tempted to think that the particular molecules that make up Kirk when he is on the ship are crucial to who he is. In order to be Kirk on the planet, he needs these molecules.

Another possible method is that the transporter dissolves Kirk but sends only the information to the planet. The transporter then assembles Kirk out of whatever materials are available. Presumably there is an ample supply of just the right organic compounds nearby. In this case, only the information is beamed down, and so we call it the "information-only method." If this method is the correct one, then it is not too much of a stretch to say that Kirk is e-mailed or faxed to the planet.

Now, knowing what you know about the transporter, how do *you* think it works? Let us look again at the information-only method. If the transporter operates in this way, what do we learn about human beings? We learn that the specific molecules that make up a person (such as Kirk) are not necessary to that person. All that is necessary to get a person is that there is enough of some material that can be put together in the right way. Let us pursue this further.

Suppose there is a malfunction in the transporter room, as usual. As the transporter gathers the material on the planet in order to re-construct Kirk, it gathers the wrong elements. Rather than building a Kirk out of carbon-based organic molecules, the transporter puts to-gether a silicon-based complex living person. The person looks like Kirk. He talks like Kirk, and he acts poorly like Kirk. Is he still Kirk?

Stop for a minute here and come up with an answer. What do you think about the silicon captain? Is it our beloved Kirk? If you think so, why do you think so? If you do not, why don't you? If your an-swer is correct, what is it that we learn about human beings?

Now what happens when Kirk is beamed back to the *Enterprise?* Does the transporter then bring together the original molecules and reassemble Kirk by using the information? In this case, Kirk again has his original body. Of course, if the information-only method is cor-rect, we do not need to use Kirk's original molecules. We can use anything we have lying around, as long as the material is adequate for organizing a person according to the complex information that makes up our illustrious captain.

If we do not need the original molecules, what do we do with them? Suppose Kirk is beamed to the planet and the ship's doctor, Dr. McCoy ("Darn it, Jim. I'm a doctor, not an actor"), decides to put Kirk's original molecules back together while Kirk is on the planet smooching some alien disco queen half his age. McCoy retrieves the information from the transporter and constructs Kirk in his lab. So now it seems that we have Kirk on the planet, torn between love and the prime directive, and Kirk in McCoy's office, filling our federation requisition forms. Only one of these survivors can be the very same person as the original. Which is the real Kirk?

Until McCoy got ambitious, it seemed obvious that Kirk was on the planet. Does the real Kirk suddenly appear on the ship even though there is a Kirk-like person on the planet? It does not seem possible that it is Kirk on the planet until the point in time at which McCoy finishes his little project. Suddenly the alien-smoocher is no longer Kirk. Kirk is back on board the ship.

What if McCoy takes the information and uses other materials (not the original Kirk molecules) and makes three or four Kirks, each of whom gives impassioned speeches about love and meaning and about how it is intrinsically valuable to be human? Well, the show's ratings would take a nosedive since we can all take only so much of that sort of dribble. But besides that, would there be three or four Kirks?

Maybe information is not enough. Let us think about the information-and-guts method instead. Let us suppose that the transporter sends Kirk's actual molecules in addition to all of the pertinent information. Then the machine reconstructs Kirk on the surface of the planet out of his original molecules. Since all of Kirk's molecules are back together in all of the right ways, not many people are going to think that it is not Kirk on the planet. After all, who else could it be?

Of course, we might get a different kind of malfunction. What if the transporter sends 100 percent of the information but only 80 percent of the molecules make it to the planet? (The rest are lost with Kirk's luggage.) So the transporter puts together a whole person, but only 80 percent of the molecules are Kirk's originals. Would the person on the planet be Kirk? Would he be 80 percent Kirk? If he is only 80 percent Kirk, who is the other 20 percent? If you think, rather, that the person would be Kirk, what percentage of the original molecules is necessary in order to get the same person? Is it 51 percent?

Now we thicken the plot a little. (Can't you hear the music building in the background?) Suppose all of Kirk's body gets reassembled but all of the information in his brain is that of Mr. Spock. So he looks like Kirk but has all of Spock's memories and mental states. Is the person Kirk or Spock? Is it Kirk with a brain transplant or Spock with a body transplant?

Let us leave Kirk on the planet with his identity questions and reflect for a minute. Philosophy, I propose, is the rational investigation of the most basic questions. Now in true philosophical fashion, we must ask what I mean by "rational investigation" and by "the most basic questions." First, let us think about basic questions. I must admit right off that a lot of the questions with which philosophers are concerned are not basic at all. Some are quite technical. Even these technical questions, I think, are raised in the context of basic questions. The most basic questions are the ones for which most people have no patience. So philosophy begins for some when most people say, "That's a stupid question."

You see none of the questions that we raised about the transporter were about the mechanics of the machine. They were all about what it means to be the same person after undergoing some change. Another way to phrase it is to ask what *the identity conditions* are for being the same person. Questions about the identity conditions for people are not raised only in science fiction. Sometimes they are closer to home.

I have three children. My oldest child is David, who turned seventeen in July 2004. I am convinced that he is the same person who turned two in 1989. But what makes him the same person? All of the molecules in his body have been replaced since his second birthday, with the possible exception of a few molecules in the center of his brain. In fact, now he has a whole lot more molecules than he did in 1989.

It is not that I do not think he *is* the same person. I want to know what *makes* him the same person. If I can figure out the answer to this question, I will learn some basic things about people. When I think hard about this question, I realize that it is difficult to come up with a satisfying theory that will explain what makes it the case that David is the same person as the two-year-old who lived in my house in 1989.

Do you know what? This issue is the kind of thing that drives philosophers. If you study philosophy, you will have a love/hate relationship with unanswered questions. On the one hand, unanswered questions bother you. They tease you. They lead you on. You struggle with them and you will consider any number of crazy answers in order to find one that will fit. Because you will not be satisfied with glib answers that avoid the difficulties in the question, you will be your own worst critic. You will be as anxious to find holes in your own ideas as anyone else.

On the other hand, you must be patient with unanswered questions. You must learn to live with them because you *will* live with them. Each question you *can* answer will spawn a dozen more questions you *cannot*. You will have to make peace with this situation. The philosopher is hounded by the unanswered question. Yet she takes delight in the very things that nag her. I think you might have at least a hunch by now of what I mean by "the most basic questions."

What do I mean by a "rational investigation" into these questions? Well, we are interested in figuring out what is *true* about the world or human nature or God or moral reality. But we are not interested simply in the best answers. We also want to find *good reasons* for thinking that these answers are the best. This is why studying philosophy is different from studying physics. In physics you learn the answers. In philosophy you learn the questions, and you learn what answers have been given in the past. You might start with some great philosopher's answers, but you only begin there. Your own investigation begins where other philosophers' investigations have ended.

In physics, you do not learn Stephen Hawking's theory about black holes in order to figure out what *you* think about black holes. You learn Hawking because he is the authority. In fact many of the reasons he has for thinking his theory is right are beyond the ability of undergraduate physics students (and many philosophy professors) to understand. We cannot understand them. So we learn Hawking's theory, and we take it on good authority that it is the best theory going. Maybe in your doctoral research in physics, you will challenge his reasons for holding his theory. Most likely, it would take years of intense research before you could challenge him successfully.

Philosophy is different in this regard. From your very first philosophy course, you may challenge the experts. You may disagree with their conclusions and with their reasons. We do not dismiss thinkers like Thomas Aquinas, Augustine or David Hume because they are antiquated. They are certainly among the greatest thinkers in history. We learn to criticize their work in order to continue their projects.

In philosophy, you do not do lab experiments. You do not have to wear lab coats and you need no protective eye gear. You do not need a million-dollar government grant to begin your investigation. There is no expensive equipment. All you need are some books, a pad of paper, a pencil and a quart or two of coffee. A philosophy lab, if there is such a thing, consists of a rubber pad on which you place your elbow so you can comfortably rest your chin in your hand as you ponder the basic but difficult questions.

We do not have labs, but we do have tools. Three especially come to mind. First, we use *logic* to evaluate arguments. In order to criticize a line of argument or to construct your own, you have to know what *kinds* of arguments are good and what kinds are bad. The difference between a good argument and a bad one has nothing to do with what the conclusion of the argument is. A good argument is one that supports its conclusion.

Second, we use *conceptual distinctions* to maintain rigorous clarity. One of the virtues to which a philosopher aspires is clarity. As a result, philosophers pay a good deal of attention to how they use their words. Philosophers must use words clearly and with precise meanings in mind. We use our words precisely in order to make our concepts clear. One question you will hear a lot is, what do you mean by that?

Third, we consult the *history of philosophy* to discover insights, mistakes and connections we would not discover on our own. Often we learn more from the mistakes a philosopher makes than we do from what we think is right about his work. Knowing both why a mistaken view was put forward and why we think it is mistaken gives us insight into how other smart people approached the problems we are facing.

Now, even after all I have said, I have not addressed the question many ask. The question is, why study philosophy? Well, why study anything? I want you to do an informal survey. Over the next few weeks ask as many students as you can what they want to study. Next ask them, "Why do you want to study this subject?" Listen to the reasons students give for choosing their course of study. Figure out the percentage of people who justify their choice on purely economic grounds. What I mean is this. When you *first* ask the question, "Why do you want to study that?" is their immediate answer something about high salaries, a good chance at a good job and job security? None of the people who answer in these ways is a philosopher. Studying philosophy is not likely to bring you any of these things.

There are, however, some pragmatic reasons to pursue studying philosophy. Some of these reasons might even bring good jobs and things like that. First, if you study philosophy, you will learn how to think. Second, if you study philosophy, you will learn how to write. And third, if you study philosophy, you will be exposed in some detail to the greatest minds in history.

Will you get a better job and make more money? Maybe and maybe not. But these reasons are good pragmatic reasons to study philosophy. And to be honest, I have to get these out of the way in order to get to the real reason to study philosophy. The *main* reason to study philosophy is singularly unpragmatic.

You might be the sort of person who finds this chapter intriguing. You might *like* the idea of chasing down questions that many people find obvious. You *want to know* what reasons there are for and against certain basic ideas. If you do, you may enjoy taking a few philosophy classes in college. You may even want to major in philosophy.

You might be another sort of person. You might be the sort that will study philosophy because you have to. You will come down with a bad case of the disease and you will not be satisfied with four years of study. For you, there is no cure. There is, however, a place to find support. If you get a bad case of the disease, you will go through five to seven years (or maybe ten) of graduate school, and I will see you at the national conference of the *American Philosophical Association.*

Be sure to say hi.

3

YOU CANNOT PROVE GOD'S EXISTENCE

If we are going to be philosophers, we ought to consider some important things that many people assume about the whole project of thinking about God. In this chapter we will look at one common idea. This is the idea that *you cannot prove the existence of God*. Have you ever heard anyone say this sort of thing before? Perhaps the person who said it was you. It is quite common for people to insist that it is impossible to prove the existence of God. In fact this claim has been elevated to the level of dogma such that it cannot be questioned. The reason I know this claim is considered unquestionable dogma is the reaction I get when I do question it. When someone says, "You cannot prove the existence of God," I want to ask, "How do you know? You just met me! How do you know what I can do? Maybe I *can* prove that God exists!"

What do most people *mean* when they say that you cannot prove the existence of God? This question is worth thinking about because when people make this claim, they are saying something important. They rarely know what it is that is important about what they are saying. I suspect someone who says that you cannot prove the existence of God thinks she is saying something important about *God*. She is not saying anything important about God, but she is saying something important nonetheless. Most people who make this claim mean something like this: *You cannot provide reasons for thinking God exists that are so good that they will convince all thinking people.* It is impossible, so the story goes, to provide a philosophical argument that is so strong or so good that everyone will be convinced. If my argument will not convince the strongest atheist, I have not proven God's existence. Since I cannot convince such an atheist to believe, my arguments do not count as proof.

Now, I agree with nearly everything here. I agree that I cannot provide an argument for God's existence that will convince all thinking people. But what does this tell me? Does this tell me anything about God? No. Does this tell me whether or not it is reasonable to believe in God? No. This tells me a lot about the nature of proof but very little about whether God exists. I cannot provide an argument that will convince everyone, without a possibility of reasonable doubt, that God exists. That is no problem. You see, I cannot provide an argument for *any* interesting philosophical conclusion that will be accepted by everyone without the possibility of reasonable doubt.

For example, I cannot prove beyond the possibility of doubt—in a way that will convince all philosophers—that the Rocky Mountains are really *there*. What I mean is that I cannot prove that the Rockies exist such that they are independent of my mind or your mind. In the same way, I cannot prove that the entire universe did not pop into existence five minutes ago and that all of our apparent memories are not illusions. I cannot prove that the other people you see in school have minds. Perhaps they are very clever robots. (How do you know that they are not?)

It is not that I cannot give arguments to support each of these ideas. What I am trying to say is that all of these arguments have parts that are less than certain. These arguments can be rationally doubted. Another way to say this is that there have been philosophers who have rejected some of the parts of each of these arguments and thus have concluded that we cannot be certain that the conclusion of the argument is true.

In fact, I have yet to encounter an interesting philosophical conclusion that can be proven beyond reasonable doubt. So the fact that arguments for the existence of God do not produce this kind of certainty (we can call it "unquestionable certainty") does not by itself weaken the case for God's existence. It simply places the question of God's existence in the same category as other philosophical questions such as that of the existence of the external, mind-independent world and the question of how we know other people have minds.

Some philosophers have thought that if it was possible to shed doubt on one part of an argument, then the whole argument was no good. I think that this assessment is not right. Are arguments for the existence of God useless? Not at all. Sure, I cannot provide an argument which will convince all thinking people that God exists, but this fact does not mean that I don't have good reason to believe in God. In fact some of my reasons for believing in God may be persuasive to you. And even if you aren't persuaded to believe that God exists, my arguments may not be useless. It is reasonable to believe that the mountains are real and that our memories are generally reliable and that other minds exist. It is reasonable to believe these things even though they cannot be proven with unquestionable certainty. Even if the arguments for God's existence do not convince you that God exists, they still may persuade you that it is *reasonable* to believe in God. So, while you might not believe in God as a result of the reasons I give, you may begin to think that it is reasonable for those who do believe in God to do so.

The big questions about God are ones like the following: Does God exist? What is God like? Are there good reasons to think that God exists? Are there good reasons to think God does not exist? What can God do? What can God know? One thing we ought to notice from this discussion is that, even if we cannot prove the existence of God, this fact makes no difference at all to any of the big questions. Once we see that it makes no difference, we can begin to think clearly about God without being distracted by what turns out to be a side issue.

4

WHAT ABOUT FAITH?

Thinking about God might be fine, but where does faith come in? Isn't it the case that we *believe* in God (supposing that we do) rather than *think* about him? Well, I do believe in God. Why, then, do I insist that we also think about God? Isn't belief enough? I guess it depends on what we mean by "enough." Enough for what? Belief in God is enough to make you a believer. Thinking about God makes you something else as well. It makes you a thinker. Of course, it is possible to think about God and not believe in him. You can be a thinker without being a believer. You can also be a believer without being a thinker. There is a third possibility as well. You can be a believer without being a *believer*. You can believe that God exists without caring very much about God or without making him a major part of your life. In this sense, you are a believer (you have the belief), but you are not a *believer* (you do not hold that belief as central to your life). Another way to make this distinction is that you can believe *that* God exists without believing *in* God. Believing that God exists is holding that a certain claim is true ("There is a person whom we call 'God'"). Believing in God is trusting in God and making him central to your life. The word *believer* has different senses and is, therefore, ambiguous.

So you can be a thinker without being a believer and a believer without being a *believer*. You can also be a believer (or a *believer*) without being a thinker. It is possible to keep all of these concepts apart from each other. Even though we can keep the concepts apart, I think the best thing is to practice all of them. It is best, so I say, to be a *believer* and to be a thinker. If you are a *believer,* I think, you ought to be a thinker as well. There are several reasons I hold this view.

First, if there is anything worth thinking carefully about it is the creator of the universe. If we take seriously the thought that God might be real and that he might have made the universe, including human beings, we have to consider that the answers to many important questions are tied up in what is true about God. For example, what is important in life? Is there any overall purpose to my life? Do I have moral or spiritual obligations? Questions like these must be related to the thoughts and purposes of God, if we think God exists.

Another reason to be a thinker is that there are not so many *believers* around. At least the general stream of our culture is such that *believers* are not taken too seriously. We want to be good thinkers because we want to be able to answer the cultural challenges to our beliefs. These challenges are often phrased as slogans: for example, "You cannot prove the existence of God." Now we already discussed this statement, but I want to add a few things. In the last chapter, I asked what a person means by this claim. Sometimes, I think, people use this claim as a conversation stopper. It is made as if merely saying it shows that nothing more is to be said. Using a claim as a conversation stopper is using it as a slogan. Our culture is full of slogans that are challenges to thinking about God or to believing in God. In fact, the slogans in our culture can be challenges to thinking at all. One set of slogans includes the sentences that begin with "Who's to say . . .": for example, "Who's to say which actions are right and which are wrong?" or "Who's to say which religion is correct?" Notice two things. First, this sentence has the form of a question. Second, it is not used as a question. It is quite rare for someone to make a "who's to say" statement and then wait for an answer. If it is a question, maybe there is an answer. One of the reasons we want to be thinkers—whether we are believers or not—is that we do not want the discussion about God or morals or reality or meaning in life to be left at the level of a slogan. If we think, we can recognize a mere slogan when we encounter it. If we think well, we can help others recognize a statement as being a mere slogan. We want to go beyond slogans and try to figure out what is true.

A third reason to be a thinker is that thinking and faith go hand in hand. They have always done so. Sometimes we get the idea that thinking is opposed to faith. The more I think, the less faith I have; or if I have faith, I can close my ears to whatever questions are in the air and just believe. There have always been certain thinkers who promoted this kind of separation between faith and thinking because they were concerned that thinking always led to the loss of faith. The history of Christian thinking tells another story as well. Rather than separating faith and thinking, many thinkers combined them. A phrase that captures how these people thought about this combination is "faith seeking understanding." Let us consider what it means to operate under faith seeking understanding. Anselm is famous for holding this method. He lived in the eleventh century. This attitude is not original with him. It finds a worthy predecessor in the life and works of Augustine, who lived from 354 to 430.

Now what did Augustine and Anselm and others mean by the phrase "faith seeking understanding"? For one thing, they thought that they *knew* certain things by faith in a reliable authority. In other words, the opposition of faith to understanding was not an opposition of opinion to knowledge. Rather, they *knew* things by means of faith on the basis of the authority of the Scriptures or the church. They sought to understand these things on the basis of reason. In this way their knowledge by means of faith would become knowledge by means of understanding. Authority as the basis for knowledge would be replaced by reason as the basis for knowledge. Nowhere in the mix is there the idea that faith results only in opinions or that one should take a skeptical or hesitant stance concerning the things one learns from authority until they pass the muster of reason.

Augustine thought that the proper method of the Christian philosopher was to continue to believe what authority told him even while he sought for understanding. He held this method not because he was gullible but because he thought certain authorities, such as the Scriptures and the church, were infallible guides to truth.

Now, what happens when a thinking believer approaches a problem in the attitude of faith seeking understanding? Sometimes a thinker will begin in faith and reach a high degree of understanding. Augustine thought he had reached understanding in his treatment of the problem of divine foreknowledge and human freedom. He thought that he had achieved understanding so that not only did he believe that we were free and morally responsible and that God knows each of our future free choices, but he could *see* how both of these claims could be true.

Often, however, we cannot reach understanding by reason. Augustine's counsel, in this case, is to continue in faith. That is, to continue to hold what you know to be true on the basis of authority. Sometimes all we can attain is *faith knowledge*. It is better also to understand, but we do not know less truly or to some inferior degree if we know by means of faith in a reliable authority.

So, if you are a *believer*, you ought to recognize that you know certain things *through* your faith. Because you are not only a believer but you aspire to be a thinker as well, you apply your thinking to these things and you try to know them through your understanding. Let me give you an example.

For most of my life, I had never been to England. I knew many things about England by faith in various reliable authorities. I listened to the Beatles. I watched *Jeeves and Wooster* on PBS. I saw pictures of the English countryside. At least I was *told* that they were of the English countryside. I had read about Oxford University and how it is made up of different colleges. Did I know things about England? Yes, I did. I knew all of these things because I had faith that the books and pictures told me the truth. I knew these things about England through my believing reliable authorities. A few years ago, my wife, Jeanie, and I traveled to England and I actually saw Oxford. Now I have *understanding knowledge* of what Oxford is like. I know what the streets are like and how narrow the sidewalks are. I also know how smoky the pubs get even in the afternoon and how beautiful the spires are. My faith knowledge was turned into understanding knowledge.

Thinking about God, then, is not in opposition to believing in

God. It is turning faith knowledge into understanding knowledge. I know that God exists through faith, and as I think hard about some of the reasons to believe in him as well, I gain understanding. My knowledge of God, then, may be both through faith and through understanding. Some issues about God are such that we can make a lot of progress in understanding them. Others are more difficult. We may not reach much understanding at all. This result should not trouble us. If God is the infinite creator of the universe, we ought to expect that we will understand only a little bit of what he is like. In any case, we have seen that faith and thinking need not be in tension with one another.

5

CAN WE BE NEUTRAL?

I let it slip out in the last chapter. I believe in God. It is true. I have been a believer for most of my life. I suppose I toyed with atheism or agnosticism when I was fourteen or fifteen, but not for long. I have been a *believer* since I was sixteen years old. It is not that I have not played around with atheism and agnosticism occasionally since then, but even in the midst of such playing, I have been a *believer*. But how can a believer (much less a *believer*) write a book on *thinking* about God? Am I not hopelessly biased? How can I hope to approach the topic in an open-minded way? I take these questions to be pretty important. There are some people who think that if I already believe, I cannot be neutral or open-minded. There are two issues here. The first question is, If I already believe, can I be neutral? The second question is, If I already believe, can I be open-minded? I think the answers are no and yes, respectively. Let us turn to the first question first. Perhaps the reason we call it the *first* question is that we deal with it *before* we deal with the other.

If I already believe, can I be neutral? I think the answer is no. It is not, however, because I already believe that I cannot be neutral. I do not think that I could be neutral even if I did not believe. I think that there is almost no one who can be neutral. I think people (believers and nonbelievers) can be *fair* and can be *open-minded*. (I will discuss being open-minded in a little while.) I do not believe very many of us can be neutral. The reason I think that we cannot be neutral is that we *are* not neutral. We have ideas and opinions and beliefs about the question we are discussing. Everybody already has some ideas about questions relating to God. In fact, we all have positions on lots of questions and, as a result, we are not neutral about those things.

OK, I am exaggerating a bit. I guess I could be neutral about something if I had no opinion or information about it at all. Hardly anyone is neutral about God, however. This lack of neutrality is not a feature that is limited to thinking about God. I think there are many important issues about which very few people are actually neutral. I think very few people are neutral about whether or not there are moral obligations or whether life is meaningful or worth living. Everyone, you see, has a philosophy of life. Let me explain what I mean by this claim. It is probably obvious to you already that not everyone is a philosopher. Not everyone, for that matter, is a thinker. I still claim that everyone has a philosophy of life. What I mean is that each person (well, maybe not young children, but anyone over nine years old) has some idea of what she thinks the world is like. I do not mean only that she has an idea about the physical world, although that is certainly the case. I am saying that everyone has some opinions about whether or not God exists or whether there are actions that are right or wrong or whether life has any meaning beyond the pursuit of pleasure. If you took someone's answers to these questions and added them up, you would get a bit of her philosophy of life. It is true that many people have not thought much about these things but, nevertheless, they have some opinions.

A second claim, I think, is related to this first claim. It is perhaps more controversial. Not only does everyone have a philosophy of life, but every philosophy of life makes *exclusive truth claims*. This second claim follows from what a philosophy of life *is*. A philosophy of life is, at the minimum, a group of ideas or claims about various aspects of reality. To have a philosophy of life is to believe certain things (in other words, to take them to be true), and to believe certain things is to think other things are false. If I think that something is true, I must think that something is false. Any true claim is such that its opposite is not true. So, merely by having a belief, I believe some exclusive truths. My philosophy of life includes things I believe. As a result, it makes exclusive truth claims.

It is an odd thing, but it is not polite today to admit that we hold exclusive truth claims. That is why you hear people say things such as "I am not saying that I am right, but . . ." or "That may be true for you, but it is not true for me." Now if you tell me something and then say, "I am not saying that I am right," what am I supposed to do? If you *think* you are right, why do you say that you are not *saying* that you are right? If you do not think you are right, why do you make the claim in the first place? Of course, there are times when we put a claim out to test it. In these cases it is perfectly all right to say that we are not saying we are right. In many normal conversations, people say, "I am not saying that I am right" when they really do think they are right.

Why don't we like to admit that we think we are right? It is true that we *do* think we are right. If I did not think my opinions were right, I would not hold them. Now, at the same time, I know that I am wrong about a lot of things. The problem is that I do not know which of my opinions are the wrong ones.

Saying something is true for one person but not for another is also very common. I do think there are a few ways in which it is perfectly fine to say that something is true for one person but not for another. The first is when it is a matter of personal preference. If I say, as I do from time to time, that butter pecan is the best flavor of ice cream, you are perfectly reasonable to say that this claim is true for me. What you mean is that it is my opinion that butter pecan is the best and that there really is no fact of the matter about which flavor is the best beyond people's preferences. The second way something can be true for me but not for you is when a certain claim is true *of* me but not of you. For example, it is true of me that I am married to Jeanie. It is not true of you. So you might say the claim "I am married to Jeanie" is true for me but not for you. A third way the phrase "true for me but not for you" is applicable is when it is used as shorthand and what is meant is that some people agree and others disagree about the claim. This situation certainly is common.

In most other areas, if something is true, then it is true for anyone even if others do not think it is true. People disagree about what is true, but when there is a disagreement, someone is mistaken. Two people cannot believe opposite things and both be right. It might be that both have different but incomplete parts of the true story, but they cannot have contradictory stories that are both true.

So I cannot be neutral. I already think some things are true and others false. I already think, for example, that God exists. I already think that those people who believe that there is no God are mistaken in their beliefs. I cannot be neutral. I can, however, be fair. I can, I think, be open-minded.

What does it mean to be open-minded? I have heard many people claim to be open-minded and more still talk about how important it is to be open-minded. One thing I have never heard any of these people explain is exactly what it takes to be an open-minded person. Let me tell you what I think it means and you can weigh my explanation. I think a person is open-minded about some issue if she identifies her assumptions and opinions about the issue and is willing to subject her assumptions and her opinions to critical inquiry.

Why is this posture an open-minded posture? It is open-minded because it pays attention to three things. We have already talked about the first two. The first is that we all have sets of beliefs even before we begin our thinking. The second is that these sets of beliefs are, most likely, not all true. The third thing this posture pays attention to is that we want to figure out what is true. So an open-minded person recognizes that she has a set of beliefs or assumptions. She then tries hard to figure out what those assumptions are and opens them up to criticism. The criticism can come from herself or from other people or both.

It is not the case that, in order to be open-minded, you must not believe some things are true and others false. An open-minded person is willing to think hard about arguments *against* her own opinions. After all, a good argument against some opinion I already have is a great tool for helping me come to the truth. Perhaps my opinion will be shown by the argument to be weaker than I thought it was (and then I can revise or reject it), or perhaps my opinion can meet the argument and I can have even more confidence that it is right (or at least in the right ballpark). It may be that I will have to postpone judgment until I can think about the topic in more detail.

A lot of people are worried about open-mindedness, I think, because they believe that people who think they are right will be arrogant and rude. I suppose some people who think they are right *are* arrogant and rude. No one wants to be arrogant and rude. I certainly do not want to be. It is not thinking you are right that makes you rude, however. I have, to be sure, talked with people who think they are right who are arrogant and rude. I have also talked with some people who think that there is no such thing as truth at all who were arrogant and rude as well. The way to avoid being arrogant and rude is not to hold the strange position that there is no such thing as truth (which, by the way, is itself an exclusive truth claim). The way to avoid being arrogant and rude is to treat people with respect. We can treat each other with respect even if we disagree about God or politics or sports or even ice cream. In fact, I think respect *requires* that I admit to you when I think that I am right and that you are mistaken. After all, I am not treating you with much respect if I pretend we do not disagree when we do disagree.

Letting you know we disagree is part of showing respect, and it can help me be open-minded. After all, if I admit to you that I believe things that you don't, I can invite you to subject my beliefs to critical scrutiny. We can help each other think better about our own beliefs. You might even be able to persuade me to change my mind. I invite you to try to do so because I want to know what is true. Disagreement and polite discussion are some of the great opportunities to make progress.

Whatever position you hold, there will always be lots of arguments against it. In fact, nearly *every philosophical claim* in this book is controversial. Let me tell you what I mean. I was giving a lecture at Ohio University on the problem of evil, and I made this confession to the audience. Afterward, a student challenged my claim that what I was saying was controversial. "I have heard all of this before," he said. What he thought I meant about being controversial was that I was going to present some new ideas that would radically break new territory in the philosophical world. Well, I can assure you that I did not break any new territory. No, when I admit that what I am going to write is controversial, what I mean is that there are smart philosophers who disagree with almost every claim in this book. In fact, there are hundreds of pages in the philosophical journals covering almost every point in each of our chapters.

I am not going to try to be neutral in this book. As I said, I do not think I can be neutral. I am not going to refrain from telling you when I think an argument is pretty strong. I will also tell you when I think an argument is pretty weak. My aim in this book is to try to present the arguments fairly and to give the beginning of a good defense for what I think is true. I think I can do both. You, however, will have to judge. So, do not be surprised if you find places where you disagree with me. Disagreement is part of doing philosophy.

6

WHERE DO WE BEGIN?

Once we have straightened out the various issues we have discussed in this section, we are ready to start our thinking about God. Up until now, to be honest, we have not been thinking about God. We have been thinking about thinking about God. We have to do this thinking in order to start thinking well about God (which is not the same as thinking well *of* God). Where do we begin? I find it helpful to zoom back the lens a bit and get a sense of what roads are possible. Where *could* we begin?

In thinking about God, we can begin in either of two ways. First, we can begin by thinking about whether there are good reasons to believe that God exists (and whether there are good reasons to think God does not). Second, we can begin by thinking about what God will be like, if there is such a being. Both of these starting points have a lot to commend them. So we could begin at either place. We will start, however, with questions about whether there is such a being as God and move on to questions about what God is like. There are a few reasons for starting in this way.

The first reason, I am afraid, involves a small confession. I know this book is called *Thinking About God,* but it is not only about this topic. I have other goals in mind besides helping you think about God. In fact, I gave hints about my goals in chapter one. My other goals have to do with helping you to think and to think better. This book is, after all, a philosophy book. A discussion of whether or not there are good reasons to think God exists is a good place to learn to do philosophy. And we do philosophy by thinking well. So one reason I will begin with the question of whether God exists, is that it is a good place to begin to do philosophy.

Another reason to begin in this way is that we all have some idea of what God will be like. Even though it is true that there are many disagreements about what God is like, we can start with a general sketch and then fill in the details later. Sketching in the details will build on the skills and information we acquire while we think about God's existence.

So we will begin with talking about whether there are good reasons to think God exists and whether there are good reasons to think that God does not. We will take the next two sections of the book to discuss these topics. The next section will be on reasons to think God does exist. The third section will be on the biggest reason to think that he does not. (I will not tell you what it is. I want you to figure out what it is on your own. You can look at the section or the table of contents to find whether your guess was right.) The fourth section will take up the question, what is God like? Now if you go through sections two and three and decide that you think that there is no person such as God, it will still be fruitful to read through the section on what God is like. For one thing, even though you do not think God actually exists, you may think that it is reasonable to think that he does. In this case, the final section will help you grasp what people who think God does exist are actually saying. For another thing, it is an opportunity to do more philosophy. Third, if I take the trouble to write that section of the book, I kind of want you to read it.

PART TWO

STARTING AT THE BEGINNING

WHY IS THERE ANYTHING AT ALL?

Why is there something rather than nothing? Have you ever thought about this question? It does not seem as though there *had* to be something. If you consider most of the things you see every day, they are all pretty much things that do not *have* to exist. In fact we can imagine very easily how they might not have existed. If my parents had never met (if my father had not gone to college in Boston, for instance), I would not have existed. My children would not have existed and there would be much less junk in our basement.

How do I know that I might not have existed? One clue is that there was a time when I did not exist. I came into existence a while ago. I am not going to tell you how long ago, but it was before microwave ovens and home computers. So I came into existence. Most of the things we see about us are things that came into existence.

Why do things come into existence? Well, there are always various reasons. Nothing comes into existence without some reason. Or at least it *seems* like nothing comes into existence without some reason. When he was ten or eleven, my middle son, Nick, caused something to come into existence. He made a dragon out of modeling clay. He called it Smaug after the dragon in *The Hobbit*. The making of a dragon is what we call an *event*. It is a happening. It is something that happens. Any time something comes into existence, an event happens. Some events are cases of things coming into existence. Sometimes they are changes in something already existing. Other events are things going out of existence. Events of all kinds happen.

In fact, events are the only things that happen. Usually they are caused to happen by other events. The dragon's being made was caused by the pressure from Nick's hands on the soft clay. Sometimes one event is both a change and a coming into existence. For example, when Nick worked with the clay, he caused a change in the shape of the hunk of clay, and at the same time he caused the dragon to come into existence.

So, many of the things we see are the kinds of things that come into existence. Part of any *complete* answer to the question of why something exists will include the things that caused it to come into existence.

Can we ask the question, why is there anything at all? I just did ask it. But can we think about it for a minute? Let us begin to think about this question by taking the universe as a whole. Why is there a universe in the first place? If the universe came into existence, then part of the answer to this question involves whatever brought it into existence. If the universe did not come into existence (that is, if it always existed), then the answer to why it exists will not involve any cause that brought it into existence.

You can probably see where I am heading. If we can show that the universe came into existence, then we have to think about what caused it to come into existence. This may be a clue to the question of whether or not God exists. Let us follow this line of thinking. Things that come into existence, we have said, are caused to exist by something else. Let's put this claim out in the open so we can see what might follow from it.

1. Whatever comes into existence is caused to exist by something else.

There are lots of things that come into existence, so we will have lots of causes. It will not do simply to have a bunch of causes randomly scattered about. We need to have chains of causes or series of causes. The coming into existence of the dragon was caused by the clay being molded into the right shape. The molding of the clay was caused by the boy's fingers and palms exerting the right kind of pressure. The exertion of pressure by the hands was caused by the arm muscles and nerves operating in the right way. The operating of the muscles and nerves was caused by Nick himself. You can see that we get a series of causes. Notice that in the series of causes, some involve changes and some involve things coming into existence.

How far back will a series of causes go? Either it can go back forever or it cannot. In other words, either the series of past causes is infinite or it is finite. If it is infinite, then for every part of the series, there is something else in the series that is previous to it and which is its cause. If it is finite, then there is some point where the whole series began. In other words, the series itself came into existence. We can capture this last thought with the following sentence:

2. If the series of past causes is not infinite, then the series of past causes came into existence.

The clincher is that no series of causes can be infinite. I will explain why this is the case in a minute. First, let us put it into a sentence so the argument can be constructed.

3. There cannot be an infinite series of past causes.

If sentences 2 and 3 are true, then we can come to a conclusion.

4. Therefore, the series of past causes came into existence.

If sentences 1 and 4 are true, then we can come to a further conclusion.

5. Therefore, there exists a cause for the series of past causes, and this cause did not itself come into existence.

I want to pull these five statements together into an *argument*. If you are going to do philosophy, you will have to get used to arguments. I do not mean that you will have to get used to screaming and throwing things. No, that is not the sort of argument that philosophers discuss. An argument is a series of statements that are put forward to support a conclusion. So our argument is the following:

1. Whatever comes into existence is caused to exist by something else.

2. If the series of past causes is not infinite, then the series of past causes came into existence.

3. There cannot be an infinite series of past causes.

4. Therefore, the series of past causes came into existence.

5. Therefore, there exists a cause for the series of past causes, and this cause did not itself come into existence.

Notice that there are three statements that do not begin with the word *therefore* and two that do begin with this word. The sentences that begin with the word *therefore* are *conclusions*. Sentence 4 is a preliminary conclusion and sentence 5 is the conclusion of the argument. This conclusion is the sentence that I am trying to get you to believe. It is the sentence the argument is supposed to prove. Now not all conclusions will begin with the word *therefore*. The other three sentences are the ones that are supposed to make it clear that the conclusion is true. These sentences are called *premises*.

How do we think about this argument? My goal in presenting it is to get you to believe the conclusion. Should you believe the conclusion? It depends on whether or not I have given you a good argument. There are different types of arguments. The kind we are thinking about is called a *deductive* argument. We call a good deductive argument a *proof*. In order for a deductive argument to be good, it has to pass two tests. The first test is whether the conclusion *follows from* the premises. In order to be a proof, an argument must be such that the premises lead to the conclusion without any jumps or loopholes. A deductive argument that passes this test is called a *valid* argument. (Note that the term *valid* as I use it applies only to arguments. To call someone's point in a discussion valid is to use the word "valid" in a different way than philosophers use it. I am using it in the more restricted sense.) *If* the premises are true, the conclusion *has* to be true. An argument has to be valid if it is to be a proof. Not every valid argument, however, is a proof. Consider this short valid argument.

6. All swans are bagels.

7. My car is a swan.

8. Therefore, my car is a bagel.

This argument is a valid argument. The premises support the conclusion without jumps or loopholes. *If* the premises are true, the conclusion *has* to be true. This argument is not a proof, however. What is wrong with it? Well, it is not *true* that all swans are bagels. Furthermore, it is not true that my car is a swan. If statements 1 and 2 *were* true, then we would have a proof. So the second test for a proof is whether all of the premises are true. If a deductive argument passes both of these tests, it is a proof. Consider this simple argument:

9. All human beings are warm-blooded.

10. My kids are human beings.

11. Therefore, my kids are warm-blooded.

This argument passes both tests. It is valid and the premises are true. We call an argument that is valid and that has all true premises a *sound* argument. A sound argument is a proof. Now we all know that my kids are warm-blooded! Imagine that!

Let us look again at my argument about the universe. Is it a proof? Well, see if it passes both tests. Does the conclusion follow from the premises? I think that it *is* a deductively valid argument. In other words, if the premises are true, the conclusion is true. You can see that there are no loopholes. If everything that has come into existence is caused to exist by something else and if this chain cannot be infinite, there must be some first cause that did not come into existence in the first place and thus it did not need to have something else cause it to exist.

Are the premises true? Let us take them one at a time. What of premise 1? It seems as though things that come into existence are caused to exist by something else. After all, nothing can cause *itself* to come into existence. In order to cause itself to come into existence, something would have to exist before it exists. We all know that nothing exists *before* it exists. So it looks like premise 1 turns out to be true.

Premise 2 seems to be true as well: If the series of past causes is not infinite, then the series of past causes came into existence. What it means to say that the series of past causes is not infinite is that it began somewhere along the way. If it never came into existence, then it always was and it is infinite.

This leaves us with premise 3: There cannot be an infinite series of past causes. Is this statement true? Is the series of past causes infinite? Can the universe have an infinite past? There are good reasons to think it cannot. That is, there are good reasons to think that this premise is true. First, there are philosophical reasons to think the past cannot be infinite. Second, there are scientific reasons that support this view.

Why can't the past be infinite? The answer is a bit complicated, so I will state it right out and then explain it in the best way I can. The past cannot be infinite because *it is impossible to complete an infinite series by successive addition.* What does this claim mean? Think of this mathematical question. Why is it impossible to count to infinity? The problem is not that you get bored with the counting procedure or that you eventually grow old and die. The problem is much bigger than these problems. It is impossible because, no matter how long you count, you will always be at a finite number. It is impossible to count to infinity even if you count by tens or thousands or millions. It is impossible to *complete* the task of counting to infinity. Once we get this in our minds, we can see two things, I think. We can see what I mean when I say that it is impossible to complete an infinite series by successive addition, and we can see that there are good reasons to think that it is actually impossible to complete an infinite series in this way.

One thing we must notice about the past is that it is complete. The series of past events is complete. This claim means that the entire series of past events ends now. It ends today. Tomorrow is not part of the series of past events. (It *will be* part of the past series, of course, but it *is not yet* part of it.) The series of past events does not extend into the future. It is complete at the present. If it is impossible to complete an infinite series by successive addition (as it is impossible to count to infinity) the past cannot be infinite. If the past is *finite,* that is, if it had a beginning, then the universe had a beginning. We have good philosophical reason then to reject the claim that the universe has always existed.

How good is this line of reasoning? I do have to admit that there are smart philosophers who are not persuaded by it. Some think that if we have an infinite amount of time, it might be possible to complete an infinite series by successive addition and that it is not, therefore, impossible for the past to be infinite. I do not think that this challenge works because I think completing an infinite duration of time is impossible for the same reason that counting to infinity is impossible. Yet if the past is infinite, then an infinite duration of time has elapsed. Other philosophers worry that this line of reasoning is in conflict with the idea of everlasting life. People who want to argue that God does exist do not want to do so, usually, in such a way that it rules out belief in everlasting life. I am not worried about this challenge either. Life everlasting would be a never-ending life. It would not be a life in which an infinite number of years has already elapsed. So I think this line of reasoning is pretty good.

There are some scientific reasons as well as philosophical reasons to think that the series of past causes is not infinite. I will not develop these. Rather, I will simply point them out. First, big bang theory seems to support the claim that the universe began to exist. If the origin of the universe was anything like what current theories in physics claim, the universe is not infinitely old. Rather, it had a beginning. Of course, there are lots of disagreements within or between current theories about the origin of the universe (and theories change with new ideas and new evidence), so it is wise not to rest too much on what looks like scientific support for the idea that the universe had a beginning.

The second scientific reason to think the universe is not infinitely old is the second law of thermodynamics. The second law of thermodynamics claims that the amount of usable energy in any closed system always decreases. Another way to state this law is that the disorder in any system always increases. (This disorder is called *entropy*.) The second law of thermodynamics explains why you need electricity to run your refrigerator and gas to run your car. Without a supply of energy, these things will stop running, and then you will have to stay home on Saturday night and drink warm Coke. Now let us think about the second law of thermodynamics and the universe as a whole.

The total amount of usable energy in a closed system always decreases. A closed system is one that does not get any extra energy from outside it. Since the universe is a closed system (at least if there is no God), it cannot be infinitely old. The fact that there still is usable energy in the universe shows that entropy is not complete. Therefore, these physical processes must have begun some finite amount of time ago.

We can see that we have good philosophical and scientific reasons to reject the idea that the universe has always existed. As a result, we have good philosophical and scientific reasons to think that the premise we are discussing (there cannot be an infinite series of past causes) is true. If it is true, then it looks as though the argument is a good one. Remember, we already agreed that the first two premises are true. So we have given a good argument for the claim that the universe was caused to exist by something outside it and that this thing did not itself come into existence. It must have existed forever.

Wait! Did I just contradict myself? I argued that there cannot be an infinite chain of causes but that there could be something that is infinitely old. How can both of these things be true? Before we turn to the next chapter, I want to assure you that I did not contradict myself. Although we will take up this worry a bit in chapter nine (and in more detail in section four), I ought to say a word or two about it here. There are two answers that may be given to this worry. First, it may be that the first cause is *not in time* at all. If the first cause is not a temporal thing, then it can be eternal without requiring that an infinite amount of time has passed. The other option is that the first cause is temporal but that time before the physical universe exists is something different than time after the universe exists. In this case, the first cause has existed eternally but it is not the case that an infinite amount of time has passed. Only physical time, it is argued, can be measured and counted. It makes no sense to talk about amounts of time before physical time.

What this argument has tried to show is that a chain of events or causes cannot be infinite. It is not impossible that something *exists* eternally. After all, if we thought it was impossible for something to exist forever, then we would think that the universe could not exist forever and we would go directly to our conclusion that it came into existence. Whatever the cause of the universe was, it was not simply one part of an everlasting series of events. It must have been something else. What it must have been, we shall discuss in chapter nine. In the next chapter I want to look at the argument from this chapter again to make sure we were not too hasty. Maybe the universe began to exist but was not caused to exist. We will have to think about this one.

8

STARTING AT THE BEGINNING

MUST THE UNIVERSE HAVE A CAUSE?

In the last chapter I gave an argument that the universe was caused to exist by something outside of it that did not itself come into existence. I want to look over that argument one more time. I want to look at it again to make sure we have not been too hasty in concluding that the universe must have been caused to exist by something outside of it. Here is the argument.

1. Whatever comes into existence is caused to exist by something else.

2. If the series of past causes is not infinite, then the series of past causes came into existence.

3. There cannot be an infinite series of past causes.

4. Therefore, the series of past causes came into existence.

5. Therefore, there exists a cause for the series of past causes, and this cause did not itself come into existence.

In the last chapter we saw that there are good reasons to believe that premise 3 is true, so we probably have not been too hasty about this one. Premise 1 may be the culprit. I skipped over it before by pointing out that it seems to be true. I think it does seem to be true, but perhaps there is more to be said. I am pretty sure that there is more to be said, and that is why I decided to say some of it in this chapter. So, I want to look again at premise 1: whatever comes into existence is caused to exist by something else.

We saw that nothing can cause itself to come into existence. But perhaps there is another alternative that we did not consider. Maybe it is possible for something to come into existence from nothing *without any cause whatsoever.* Can a thing just pop into existence with absolutely no cause? It is hard to know how to go about answering this question. I think it is safe to say that we do not expect, in our everyday lives, to encounter things that have popped into existence without any cause whatsoever. I fully expect there to be causes for things even if my kids often deny the existence of such causes.

For example, if I walk into our dining room and see a picture of Pinky and the Brain that has been drawn on the wall in marker—let us say it is *permanent* marker—I will ask something like, "Where did this picture come from?" It seems to me to be a reasonable question. Suppose my daughter, Elizabeth, says, "It came from nothing, Dad. Nothing caused it. It just popped into existence without any cause whatsoever. I think it is quite strange. Don't you?" Will I accept this? No, I will not. Pictures on the wall are not the sort of things that pop into existence without any cause at all.

If we think about the other kinds of things we generally encounter, then we will observe that these things as well do not pop into existence without any cause. In fact, every time we encounter some object that has come into existence, we think there was a cause of its existing. This expectation is pretty deep and constant. It is worth asking if there are any exceptions to our expectation that there will be some cause to things. Because it is worth asking this question, I will ask it. Are there any exceptions to this deep and constant expectation of ours?

Actually, there are *two* questions lurking in the neighborhood. First, are there any exceptions at all to this expectation? Second, could the universe itself be such an exception? Even now, the way I worded these questions is not quite right. We are not concerned with whether or not someone could take exception to the idea that everything that came into existence is caused to come into existence. It is surely possible that people will (and have) taken exception to this idea. We are interested in whether it is *more reasonable* to accept any exception to this idea than not to accept an exception. So I should reword my two questions: First, is it reasonable to think that there are any exceptions at all to the idea that anything that comes into existence is caused to exist by something else? Second, is it reasonable to think that the universe as a whole is an exception to this idea?

The reason we want to keep these two questions a bit separate is that having something that counts as an exception might not affect our argument very much. Even if it is reasonable to think that there are some exceptions, our argument could be adjusted to take account of these things. In order to find a loophole in our argument, we need good reason to think that the universe as a whole might be an exception to our deep and constant expectation.

You might think that I am being needlessly thorough in giving so much space to this first question. It does not appear (at least to most people) to be reasonable to think that anything can come into existence without a cause. I agree that it does not *appear* to be reasonable. It turns out, however, that these appearances may be deceiving.

It will help the discussion at this point if we switch from talking about things coming into existence to talking about things happening. What kinds of things can happen without any cause? Physicists tell us that *quantum events* can do so. A quantum event involves something like the movement of a very small subatomic particle. Current quantum theory indicates that some particles can jump from one quantum level to another in a way that is uncaused and not otherwise determined. To tell you the truth, I do not understand this very well, but I take the physicists' word for it. I rely on their authority when it comes to these very small particles. If they are correct, then some events occur without being caused to occur. This discovery is pretty amazing since it overthrows the view of the universe that most people held throughout the first three hundred years of modern science. Some things can happen without being caused to do so.

Of course, quantum events are not primarily cases of something coming into existence. They are changes in the state of a particle. Even so, if changes can occur without any cause, then the idea that something can come into existence without any cause seems more plausible than it did before. Furthermore, a change in state occurs when an old state goes out of existence and a new one comes into existence. When I set my coffee cup down somewhere and forget where it is, the coffee grows cold. When this happens, we could say that the state of my coffee's being hot goes out of existence and the state of my coffee's being cold comes into existence. If quantum events can happen without a cause, then certain states of some small particles can come into existence without a cause.

These facts about quantum physics undermine the premise we are discussing in the form we are thinking about it. Remember, the premise claims that whatever comes into existence is caused to exist by something else. If the physicists are right about quantum theory, this premise is false. There are states that do come into existence without being caused to come into existence. It still remains to be seen what these facts about quantum physics have to do with whether the universe itself can come into existence without a cause. The universe, after all, is not very like the quantum states of sub-atomic particles. They are typically quite small and the universe is a very big thing. Simply pointing out that some event does not require a cause will not give us reason to suppose that we do not need a cause for the universe. It does give us a reason to reword the premise, though. Perhaps we should say, "Really big things that come into existence are caused to exist by something else." If we think the phrase "really big things" does not sound technical enough, we might try something like "supra-atomic things and events that come into existence are caused to exist by something else." A supra-atomic thing is the opposite of a subatomic thing. Subatomic things are smaller than atoms. Supra-atomic things are bigger than atoms. This distinction might work for our purposes but it might not. If we discover that it does not, we can drop it, but I want to use it for a while since I just made it up.

Granting the subatomic exceptions to our expectations about causes, are we confident that supra-atomic things that come into existence are caused to exist? Well, I want to hesitate at this point. All of the supra-atomic things I encounter on a daily basis seem to be the kinds of things that are caused to come into existence. I do not, however, encounter a lot of things that are like the universe *as a whole*. In fact, I do not encounter the universe as a whole at all. I only encounter small chunks of it at a time. Can I go from all the different things I do encounter that are caused to come into existence and conclude that this other thing that I do not encounter also was most likely caused to come into existence? Remember, we have already agreed that the universe as a whole came into existence. Here we are worried about whether it was caused to come into existence. The universe has a lot in common with the everyday things that are caused to come into existence. It is big and it is physical, for instance. It is not something abstract like a number. It differs in striking ways from the ordinary things, however. For example, it exists but does not exist anywhere. It is spatial but it is not *in* space. It would be more accurate to say that space is *in it*. Similarly the laws of physics do not act on it as a whole. They act within it. Furthermore, although the universe is a very big thing now, it was not always so big. At the moment and slightly after the big bang, the universe was very small. In fact, it was something, at least for an instant, about the size of a subatomic particle.

Given these similarities and these differences, can we conclude that it is more reasonable to think that the universe was caused to come into existence than that it was not caused? This is the point in the discussion where it is difficult not to "beg the question." To beg the question is to assume, sometimes in a subtle way, the very thing you are trying to demonstrate. For example, someone who assumes that the universe contains all the reality there is will have a hard time thinking that it could have been caused to exist by something outside of it. Someone, like me, who already believes in God will not be troubled by this idea. Rather, I will have a hard time thinking that the universe is one of those somewhat unusual cases of something coming into existence without a cause. Are we at a standstill? I hope not.

Rather than assuming one answer or the other, suppose we try to assume that it is at least possible that the universe does not contain all of the reality there is. At the same time, let us assume, if we can, that it is possible that the universe *does* contain all of the reality there is. That is, suppose we assume that it is possible that there is a God and that it is possible that there is not. How would holding both of these assumptions bear on our wondering if the universe could have come into existence without a cause?

I will tell you what I think. I think two things. First, even after thinking about this issue for a while, I think that it *is* possible that the universe popped into existence without a cause. I can't see strong enough reason to make the claim that such a thing would be either impossible or so unlikely that it is irrational to believe. Second, I think that it is still more reasonable to hold that the universe was caused to exist than that it popped into existence without a cause. Let me tell you why. First, I think that the universe as a whole is a physical object that is pretty big and has lots of different properties. Even though it began quite small, apparently all of the matter and energy present in the universe today was concentrated in that small object. The history of the universe is a history of the expansion of all of that matter and energy. So, although it was similar in size to a subatomic particle, its properties were quite different. Granting that it is possible that the universe might have come into existence without a cause, it seems difficult to claim that it *actually* was uncaused *unless you have a reason* to think that this is what happened. There may be reasons for thinking that the universe came into existence without a cause, apart from its relatively small degree of similarity to a subatomic particle. I do not know what any of the reasons could be.

About the universe, then, there are only three alternatives:

1. The universe has always existed. It has an infinite past.

2. The universe popped into existence from nothing with absolutely no cause.

3. The universe was caused to exist by something outside it.

We have seen in the last chapter that we have pretty good reasons to reject the first alternative. In this chapter we have seen that we cannot rule out the second alternative decisively. It is possible that the universe was not caused at all. I have argued, however, that it is more reasonable to reject this alternative than to accept it. If we do so, this position leaves us with the third as the more reasonable alternative. The universe was caused to exist by something outside it. There was a first cause. This cause existed eternally. It initiated the big bang and caused the universe to come into existence. Now what can we know about this cause? Why should we think the cause is God? We will consider this important question in the next chapter.

9

STARTING AT THE BEGINNING

MUST THE FIRST CAUSE BE GOD?

In the last two chapters we have discussed an argument for the conclusion that there exists a first cause that did not come into existence. In other words, the first cause always existed. We concluded that we have fairly good reason to suppose that there was such a first cause. What, then, can we know or reasonably conclude about this cause? Why think that the cause is God?

This question is important for several reasons. One reason is historical and the other is not historical. The reason that is not historical is that showing that there was a first cause is not enough to show that God exists. It may seem obvious to you or to others that *if* there was a first cause, that cause was God. This step, though, needs some justification. Many times we think there is a cause for some event, but we do not attribute the cause to persons (either natural or supernatural). When I spot a new chunk of rust on my car I assume there is a cause for the spot of rust. Usually, though, I do not think the cause is a *person*. The cause is probably some event, such as the water and air reacting with the iron that is exposed due to a ding in my car door that I picked up in the parking lot at Stop and Shop. Do we have reasons to think the first cause is not simply another event? Why think it is a supernatural person?

The historical reason why this question is important is that many people accuse one of the great thinkers in history of simply assuming that the first cause must be God. Thomas Aquinas is best known for his famous "five ways." He argues that the existence of God can be proven in five ways, and he outlines these ways in about a page and a half. Each of Aquinas's proofs is an attempt to show the world needs a cause. Aquinas, following Aristotle, thought that there were four different types of causes and that each of them was required for a complete explanation of anything. He argues that the world needed to be caused in each of the four ways causes can operate. (For one of the four kinds of causes, he develops two different arguments; hence there are five arguments for God's existence.) At the end of each of these short arguments, he arrives at the notion of some kind of cause for the world. Then he says that this cause is God.

If Aquinas had left the discussion at this point, it would be fair to press the accusation against him. He does not leave the discussion at this point, however. Aquinas takes the next several hundred pages or so in his work to explain why the first cause must be God. These arguments are generally left out of the anthologies of the history of philosophy. The important point is that he does not *merely* state that the first cause is God. He goes on to give very detailed reasons for thinking that this claim is true.

We will not take hundreds of pages to argue from the concept of the first cause to the conclusion that God is the first cause. I do want to point out briefly, however, some reasons to think that this inference is a good one. How do we begin to think about the nature of this first cause?

Let us consider a few things about the first cause. First, it caused the entire universe to come into existence. Because of this fact, we know that the first cause is not *part* of the universe. What does it mean that the first cause is not part of the universe? Well, for one thing, the first cause is not something in space. Space is part of the universe. Everything in space is part of the universe. The cause of the whole spatial universe cannot itself be in space.

Second, the first cause is not something temporal. We looked briefly at this worry in the last chapter. Some philosophers make a distinction between *physical* time and *metaphysical* time. Physical time is part of the universe. It came into existence with the universe. Whatever caused the universe to come into existence, then, is not something in physical time. The way philosophers make this distinction is to point out that physical time is clock time. It is time that has an intrinsic metric. In other words, it is measurable. The only way time can be intrinsically measurable is if there is some event that is cyclical or repeated at given intervals. An obvious example is the rotation of the Earth. We measure our time in days because there is a regular event that can mark off the passage of time. These considerations have to do with physical time. It may be the case that without (or "before" there was) a physical universe—and hence, any physical metric—there was time. This time would be metaphysical time. It would have no measure and would be what philosophers call *amorphous.* If the first cause existed in metaphysical time, then it can be true that this cause never itself began and that it also did not exist through an infinite number of moments of time. In metaphysical time, there are not moments or amounts of time. In this way, it was not contradictory to say that there cannot be an infinite series of past causes yet that the first cause never came into existence.

Another way to think about the first cause is to think that it was not in time at all. In other words, it was *atemporal.* In this way it never began but it also does not have to live through an infinite series of moments in succession. As I promised in the last chapter, we will think about these issues more thoroughly in section four. We will put these questions to the side for now. It is enough to know that the cause of the universe is not an event in the same way that the cause of the rust on my car is an event. It is not something that occurred in measurable time.

The first cause also is not physical. Everything physical is *within* the universe. Whatever caused the universe to exist, then, is not itself physical. This claim may seem to be obvious at this point since we have already pointed out that the cause of the universe is neither spatial nor temporal. Maybe everything that is physical is spatial or temporal or both. If everything physical is spatial or temporal and if the first cause is neither spatial nor temporal, then it follows that the first cause cannot be physical.

So we have a few ideas about the first cause on the table. It is not physical. It is not in space or time. It is not part of the universe. To this list, we can add a few more items. The first cause must be something with lots of power. After all, the universe has come to be pretty big. It is spread out (literally) all over the place. No small cause could kick off such a big event.

The most important implication of there being a first cause is the one I am saving for last. There is good reason to think that the first cause is a *person*. It is not simply a force but it must have aspects of personhood, namely, that it wills. It acts. How do we know this? We have good reason to think that the first cause is a personal agent because this claim provides the best answer to the question of why the universe began to exist when it did. Why not sooner? Why not later?

Let's try to think about this. Suppose the universe was caused to come into existence twenty billion years ago. The question that naturally arises is, why did it happen then and not some other time? Why did it not come into existence fifty billion years ago? Why not seventy-five? Why not three? If we ask these kinds of questions about events *within* the universe, we can always come up with a reason. For example, I told you a couple of chapters ago about Nick's making a dragon out of modeling clay. I cannot remember exactly when it actually happened, so we will suppose it was at 3 p.m. on a Tuesday. We can ask, why did it not come into existence at 2 p.m.? Why not on Wednesday?

These kinds of questions have good answers. The dragon did not exist at 2 p.m. because it was not made until 3 p.m. It was not made until 3 p.m. because Nick did not begin working with the clay until 2:30 p.m. To put these answers into a general form, we could say that the dragon was made at 3 p.m. because it was not until 3 p.m. that all the conditions were gathered at the right place for the making of the dragon. It could not be made until the clay was shaped in the right way by Nick's hands.

I know that it sounds funny to talk of fifty billion years ago if the universe—and time—is only twenty billion years old. To rephrase these sentences to be more technically correct makes them a bit cumbersome. We would have to say something like this: "If past physical time were thirty billion years longer than it in fact was, we would find the conditions for the universe's coming into existence present then as well." Or "If past time were seventeen billion years shorter than it in fact was, the conditions needed for its coming into existence would have been present throughout that timeless eternity." I will leave this cumbersome way of speaking aside for the time being. You will get to use enough of these cumbersome sentences when you go to graduate school.

We ought also to observe another fact. Once all of the conditions were gathered together, the dragon came into existence. It did not come into existence a week afterward. It came into existence as soon as the conditions were gathered together. As soon as the clay was properly shaped (right after it was pressed in the right way by Nick's hands), the dragon came into existence.

The conditions that *have* to be gathered in order for an event to happen are called the *necessary* conditions for the event. They are called the necessary conditions because they are *necessary* to the event's happening. If any of these are taken away, the event will not happen. The *sufficient* conditions for the event are those that are such that once they *are* gathered the event happens straightaway. These conditions are *sufficient,* or *enough,* to make the event happen. When we speak of the cause of some event, we usually mean the sufficient conditions. We ignore most of the conditions that are necessary but not sufficient. The clay's being shaped appropriately is a sufficient condition for the dragon to come into existence. A necessary condition for the dragon's existence is that the temperature of the clay does not instantaneously increase to 5000° centigrade. If the temperature did jump to 5000 °C, the clay would evaporate and not hold its dragon shape. We generally ignore conditions such as this one in our thinking about causes.

So we have observed that the event does not occur until both the necessary and the sufficient conditions are present. What do these observations have to do with the first cause's being a person? I will try to explain. If the universe was caused to come into existence, all of the necessary and sufficient conditions for its coming into existence were gathered twenty billion years ago. Why did the universe not come into existence fifty billion years ago? If all of the conditions were present twenty billion years ago, they would have been present fifty billion years ago.

I want you to do an experiment. Think about raising your left arm but don't do it yet. OK? Now, raise it. Why was it raised when it was? All of the conditions were present when you thought of raising it. If you had *willed* to do it then, it would have been raised. All of the conditions were present but the event was initiated by your willing to raise your arm. Of course, once you will to raise your arm, a fairly complex series of events begins to occur, including the firing of brain cells and nerves and the contraction of muscles. But it is your will that initiates this series. Now hold your arm up for an hour. (Just kidding!)

You are a personal agent. You initiate events simply by your will. All of the conditions are standing by, ready. You only have to will to raise your arm and you do it. The fact that you will at one time rather than another is not itself caused by anything other than your willing. People can initiate various series of events simply by willing them. Your initiating the events that culminate in your raising your arm is not caused by some other event. Although this last claim is controversial among philosophers, I think it is true.

We can make a distinction between types of causes here. Most causes are cases of event causation. One event causes another. Most events are caused by other events. Some events, as we saw in chapter eight, are not caused at all. Others, I want to claim, are caused but they are not caused by other events. They are caused by persons. The event of your arm's going up in the air, when you will to raise it, involves a series of events, but this series is initiated by a person. You willed it.

If it is true that persons can initiate a new series of events by willing to do so, then we have another exception to our causal premise from chapter eight. The willing of a personal agent is something that happens and it is not caused by anything outside the person. This exception does not weaken the argument that the universe needs a cause because the idea that the universe was caused to exist by the will of a person is one version of the alternative for which I was arguing. That alternative is that the universe was caused to exist by something outside it. If it was caused to exist by a person who is not part of it, then it *was* caused to exist by something outside it.

So where are we? The universe's coming into existence when it did (and not at some other time) is an odd thing. The best explanation for this fact is that whatever caused the universe to come into existence did so by an act of *willing* it to come into existence. If the first cause is not a personal agent, then we cannot make much progress in thinking about why the universe is the age that it is.

If we take all of the things we have learned about the first cause and add them up, we get a description that points to a being that has many of the characteristics traditionally ascribed to God. To be sure, it does not have all of the properties we might think that God must have. The first cause is powerful, it is not physical, it is outside space and time, and it is a person. These qualities point in God's direction. They add up to good reasons to think that the first cause is God.

So, in these three chapters, we have argued that the universe came into existence, and that it is more likely that it was caused to come into existence, and that it was caused to do so by a person. How good is this argument? Is it a proof? Well, in the introduction section we discussed proofs. I do not think that this argument comes close to being a proof with unquestionable certainty. We have not shown that it is *impossible* that the universe popped into existence from nothing without a cause. Nor have we shown that the first cause *has* to be God. We have argued that it is more reasonable to hold that the universe was caused to exist and that its cause is a nonphysical personal agent. So it seems that this argument is fairly strong, as philosophical arguments go. The existence of the universe points to the existence of God.

10

LOOKING AT THE DETAILS

Suppose we are walking together across a field and I stub my toe on a rock. After the pain subsides, I might ask where the rock came from. If you answer me by saying something like, "It is just a rock. It is here, most likely, for no particular reason. It has probably been here for ten thousand years," I will accept that as a pretty good answer. Now suppose I stub my toe on a watch, say, a gold Timex with a shiny band. If you give me the same sort of answer—if you say that it is here for no reason and has probably been here for ten thousand years—I will not think your answer is very good. There is a large difference between stubbing your toe on a rock and stubbing it on a watch. For one thing, it hurts more to stub it on a rock. For another, it is more expensive to replace the watch once it is kicked.

I have to confess that the first few sentences of this chapter were pretty much plagiarized. I paraphrased a few sentences out of the book *Natural Theology*, which was published in 1802 by William Paley. He uses the analogy of the watch and the rock to point out that some objects bear the marks of being designed and others do not. The rock looks as though it is where it is, and is like what it is like, purely by accident. The watch, however, was probably lost by some person, and it surely was not put together accidentally by the action of wind and rain on dirt and grass. The watch was made by some human being for a purpose. The rock, it seems, was not.

Paley and many other thinkers have thought that this analogy fits other things we observe in the world. There are other things that bear the marks of being designed for some purpose. These things, however, were not designed by any human person. They were designed, Paley argues, by an intelligent creator.

Now why does Paley think that no human person designed the things he discusses? The answer is that some of the things he discusses are parts of human beings themselves. We know that no human being came up with the design that determined what human beings would be like. Yet, Paley thinks, human beings bear the marks of being the products of design. Consider the eye. It is a complex organ that performs a function. The function is not one that directly benefits the eye only. It is a function that benefits the whole person. It functions with a purpose. Sometimes your eyes function well and sometimes they do not.

I have pretty good eyes. When I was young, I was called on to read the signs on the highway because I could always make them out before anyone else in the car. When I was twenty-eight, I married Jeanie. Shortly thereafter, I set up an appointment with an eye doctor. I thought I needed glasses because I thought my eyes were getting worse. Jeanie, you see, could read the signs before I could. It turned out that my eyes were fine but hers were even better. My mother cannot read signs very well. She relies on others in the car to help navigate the way. So our eyes perform their function more or less well. Mine are better than my mother's. Jeanie's are better than mine.

What does it mean to say that our eyes perform more or less well? It means that the eyes have a function or a goal and they meet the goal to some degree or they do not. Now I do not want to say that reading highway signs is the goal of human eyesight. The goal is something more general, such as seeing objects around us or seeing things well enough to find food and avoid danger. If there is a purpose for the eye, though, there is some reason or design behind it. If there is a design, then there is a designer.

The kind of reasoning that we just walked through is called a *design argument*. It is an argument from something that appears to be designed to the existence of a designer. This kind of argument is, perhaps, one of the most well known kinds of arguments for the existence of God. There are many things that appear to have been designed. These things function for some purpose and they seem to function very efficiently. Furthermore, they seem to be *good* things. It is a good thing to be able to see. It is a good thing to be able to hear. Our eyes and our ears seem to be designed for these good purposes. It is good that our hearts keep pumping blood and our glands keep secreting saliva. We have many organs and systems in our bodies that work to fulfill good purposes. We are much more like the watch we stumbled on than we are like the rock against which we stubbed our toe. The marks of design are everywhere. There must have been a designer. These things could not have happened by chance.

How good of an argument is this? Before we think about the design argument as an argument, let us think about it as a *hunch*. How strong of a hunch is it? I think it is pretty strong. I think this hunch is pretty strong because we make distinctions between designed things and accidental things all of the time. If I walk out into my front yard and notice that my car is streaked with dirt, I may wonder about it but I will not generally blame anyone. After all, we hardly ever wash it. Suppose I see that the streaks are shaped like a series of letters. Suppose they are strangely shaped almost exactly like the letters in the phrase *Wash me!* In this case, I will think that someone has streaked up my perfectly dirty car. Some person made the streaks into those shapes. Now each of these hunches is pretty good. If my car is dirty and streaked with no apparent pattern, it is reasonable for me to conclude that it got dirty accidentally. If the streaks resemble letters that spell a word or sentence, it is no longer reasonable for me to think the streaks got that way accidentally.

The example of my dirty car is but one of many examples which show that we often look at things and conclude that they are not accidental. The hunch that some things are designed, rather than are the product of an accident, is a strong hunch. Can we make a good argument out of this hunch? Let us see if we can.

1. If some thing or system of things that is not made by human beings shows strongly the marks of being designed, then it was designed.

2. Many things not made by human beings show strongly the marks of being designed.

3. Therefore, they were designed.

4. Therefore, a designer who is not a human being exists.

This is a valid argument, is it not? If the premises are true, the conclusion is true and we have shown that a designer exists. Is it a sound argument? (That is, given that it is valid, are all of the premises true?) I do not think it is sound. You will want to question both premise 1 and premise 2. Right now I want to question premise 1. I will look at premise 2 in the next chapter.

I think premise 1 as it stands is false. Suppose there is something (not made by human beings) that shows strongly the marks of being designed. Must such a thing be a designed thing? I do not think so. When I was about nine, our family took a vacation through New England. We drove to Boston and then from Boston north into New Hampshire. We traveled in the White Mountains and our car climbed Mount Washington. Next we drove into Vermont and saw the Green Mountains. One interesting thing I learned is that the White Mountains and the Green Mountains were pretty much the same color. Along the way we saw an important sight. There was a place in New Hampshire called "the Old Man in the Mountain." In fact a picture of it is on the New Hampshire license plates and on the back of the commemorative quarter from New Hampshire. The Old Man in the Mountain is a rock formation on the side of one of the steep cliffs. It looks just like the profile of an old man. In fact it looks more like a person than many statues I have seen that have been carved to look like people. The odd thing is that no human person carved it. As far as we can tell, erosion, caused by rain and wind over the years, formed it. (I learned, as I was writing this book, that the rock formation has since collapsed!)

The Old Man in the Mountain is a formation that bears the marks of being designed. The problem is that it was not designed. It is a product of accidental forces. So here we have a *counterexample* to our premise. Remember that the premise claimed that if something not made by human beings bore the marks of design then that thing was, in fact, designed. Now we see that this premise is not true. So what should we do?

Well, a premise that is not true is like a broken-down car. A good philosopher will try to fix it. Fortunately for our discussion, philosophers are generally much better at fixing up premises than they are at fixing up cars. This fact explains why you never see premises jacked up on cinder blocks in front of philosophers' homes.

Let us have a go at fixing this premise. My first impulse is to resort to a common philosophers' strategy. Actually, I figured out this kind of strategy while trying to fix my car a few dozen times. We could call it the "first thing to try" strategy. With my car it goes like this: "The first thing to try is dry-gas." When trying to fix my car, the first thing I do is pour dry-gas into the tank. The philosopher's dry-gas is *probability*. If a premise is broken, see if you can fix it by inserting the word *probably* at some appropriate spot. Often, inserting *probably* makes it possible for us to get the argument jump-started.

There are various kinds of probability. The two more important kinds for our purposes can be called the "coin-flipping" kind of probability and the "for all we know" kind of probability. Coin-flipping probability has to do with calculating the odds of something occurring. Given that a coin has two sides, the probability that a flipped coin will land heads up is one in two. We are not using coin-flipping probability here. We are not interested in calculating the odds and, to be honest, I do not see how one could begin to do so. We are using the for-all-we-know kind of probability. If, as far as we can tell, something is the case, then we say it is probably the case. In the current discussion, if we insert *probably,* we get this:

1* If some thing or system of things that is not made by human beings shows strongly the marks of being designed, then it was *probably* designed.

(Note that I numbered this premise 1* to indicate that it is an adjustment to premise 1 above. Premise 1** below is a variation of premise 1*.)

So the claim is that if we find something that was not made by human beings and it looks like it was designed, then as far as we can tell it was designed. This move will not do the job. Sometimes even dry-gas won't fix the problem. The Old Man in the Mountain shows strongly the marks of design. Was it probably designed? The answer is no. We *know* that it was not designed. I think we need to do some more fixing. The Old Man in the Mountain example is instructive. We have something that shows the mark of design—or we could call it *apparent design*—but it was not actually designed. Furthermore, and this consideration is the one in which I am interested, we can tell a *story* about why this thing looks for all the world as though it was designed when it was not. It is this story that is important here. Suppose we try to bring into our premise the fact that we have such a story. We can try something like the following:

1** If some thing or system of things that is not made by human beings shows strongly the marks of being designed *and we have no fairly good story to tell about how it shows the marks of design without really being designed,* then it was probably designed.

I think this premise has a better chance at being true. Make sure you notice that I kept the word *probably* in the premise. I did this because the fact that we cannot tell a fairly good story about the marks of design does not guarantee that there is no story about this at all. We might not be aware of the story.

It looks as though we have a good version of premise 1. In order to make our argument work, now, we have to tinker with premise 2. It is not enough to say, as premise 2 does, that many things not made by human beings show strongly the marks of being designed. It is not enough that things *show* the marks of being designed. They have to show these marks and it also must be true that we cannot explain how these things got the marks of being designed in any way other than from an actual designer. In other words, it must be the case that we have no story to tell about how the thing in question got to look designed. So our premise might look like this:

2** Many things not made by human beings show strongly the marks of being designed *and we have no fairly good story to tell about how they show the marks of design without their really being designed.*

(2** is a variation of premise 2. I use the two asterisks to show that this new premise will go with 1**.)

If premise 1** is true and premise 2** is true, then we can deduce the following two claims:

3** Therefore, they were *probably* designed.

4** Therefore, a designer who is not a human being *probably* exists.

Notice that I again have to insert that word *probably*. The reason I must do so is that premise 1** only gives us a probable design. A probable design only probably gives a designer. Still, the conclusion that probably a designer exists is pretty strong. If we could show that God probably exists, we will have done a lot more than many people think can be done in this regard. I don't think we are there yet. The problem, now, is the new premise 2.

2** Many things not made by human beings show strongly the marks of being designed *and we have no fairly good story to tell about how they show the marks of design without their really being designed.*

There was a time when most thinkers thought this premise was true. Now, not many do. What do you think changed their minds? I will give you a hint. The change began in the middle of the nineteenth century. Before you read on, make a guess about what might have caused so many people to change their minds about a premise such as this one.

LOOKING AT THE DETAILS

In the last chapter we brought out an argument for the conclusion that some of the things in the universe were probably designed. Therefore, probably, a designer exists. It went as follows:

1** If some thing or system of things that is not made by human beings shows strongly the marks of being designed *and we have no fairly good story to tell about how it shows the marks of design without being designed,* then it was probably designed.

2** Many things not made by human beings show strongly the marks of being designed, *and we have no fairly good story to tell about how they show the marks of design without their really being designed.*

3** Therefore, they were *probably* designed.

4** Therefore, a designer who is not a human being *probably* exists.

There is one aspect of premise 2 that we did not discuss in much detail. What, exactly, are the things that show the marks of being designed? We alluded to things like the human eye and other organs that perform more or less well. We noted that if it is true that they perform more or less well, then there must be some purpose or plan according to which they should function. Eyes are for seeing and hearts are for pumping blood. When the eye fails to work, we no longer see. When the heart stops pumping blood, our blood pressure goes way down. The complex functioning of the organs of the body has led many thinkers to believe that they were designed with these functions in mind. They work extremely well, for the most part. (I seem to have acquired, however, a systematically malfunctioning sense of direction.)

These items are surely examples of things that show strongly the marks of purpose and design. The argument, then, seems like it is a strong one. We just need to look around to make sure there is not a story lurking nearby that explains how these things look designed when they are in fact accidental. We do not have to look too far. There is such a story and it is very widely believed.

This story, as I said, began to be popular in the second half of the nineteenth century. In the middle of that century, Charles Darwin published his famous work *On the Origin of Species,* in which he explained his theory of biological evolution through natural selection. Darwin's theory, once it became widespread, all but eliminated serious consideration of the kind of design argument we have here. The reason his book had this effect was that it provided an account of a mechanism that explained how things that looked designed could arise by accident. In other words, he came up with a story about how things could show the marks of being designed even though they were not designed.

How does Darwin's story go? Well, the important points (for our discussion) can be sketched out very simply. The story requires three ingredients. First, there must be some random distribution of variations in organisms. Second, it must be that some variations are better than others as far as survival and reproduction are concerned. Third, the variations must be, in general, hereditary. Let us look at each of these three ingredients in action. Consider frogs. Suppose there are some random variations in how frogs come out. Some are a bit larger or faster or differently colored than others. Some can see better and others have better tongues with which to catch flies. These frogs will survive more or less well. The slow ones are more likely to get eaten by snakes, and the ones with good tongues will get the most flies. And in the world of frogs, he with the most flies wins, provided he does not get eaten by a snake. The winning frogs will be more likely to have little frog babies. Since the variations are passed to the frog babies, those features that are helpful for survival get passed down through the generations. So we wind up with frogs that have all of these features that look as though they are designed to help the little slimy things survive.

Of course, Darwin's story is a bit more complicated than I let on because it involves variations from species to species. For example, some fish developed enough variations that their offspring became amphibious. Frogs or some other amphibians developed enough variations to become more independent of the water and they became reptilian. From reptiles we got birds and mammals. It took a long time and a lot of random variations. Note that not all frogs became reptiles. After all, frogs survive fine the way they are. It is good that they continue to survive because the snakes need something to eat. But the story is that all of the different species of living things emerged through the random variation and heredity and the pressure to survive.

Now I want to point out a few things about the role Darwin's story plays in the argument we are discussing. For one thing, in order for Darwin's story to undermine the strength of the argument, it does not have to be a *true* story. It only has to be *plausible*. If we can say, "Well, it looks like Darwin's story *might be* the way things happened," then premise 2 of our argument is false—or, at least, it is terribly weakened. This consideration is why I put the phrase "fairly good story" into the premises of the argument. If the story is fairly good, then it may be the case that we have things that have the appearance of design but that are accidental all the same.

Also, even if Darwin's story *is* true, it does not follow that there is no designer. After all, God might have used the mechanisms that Darwin proposed in order to get the kinds of things he wanted to get. What Darwin's story does is it shows that this *particular argument has failed*. We might have other reasons for thinking God exists, but we must admit that *this* particular line of reasoning is not very strong. Given that most biologists think that some story pretty much like Darwin's is the way things happened, this argument will not be very persuasive.

The things that looked as though they point to a designer may be accidental after all. Like the Old Man in the Mountain, eyes and hearts and lungs and frogs may have gotten their appearance of design by accidental means. The design argument for the existence of God has fallen into disrepute. In fact, many people have thought that Darwin has struck a fatal blow to any such argument. That is, they had this opinion until very recently.

Think about Darwin's story for a minute. Is there any hope of making the kind of argument we are discussing work even with Darwin's story? Remember that Darwin's story requires heredity. It works, then, for things that reproduce. As far as we know only living things reproduce. Dead things do not, and neither do inorganic things such as rocks and stars and water molecules. If there were nonliving things that showed apparent design, we might be able to resurrect a version of the design argument that may be immune from Darwin's story. It turns out that there is such a thing, and it has been discovered only very recently how it shows apparent design. We will look into what this thing is in the next two chapters.

12

LOOKING AT THE DETAILS

FINE-TUNING AND DESIGN

We ended the last chapter with the desire to find things that have the appearance of design but that are not living. We saw, remember, that arguments from the appearance of design in living things or in parts of living things to the existence of a designer are quite weak. The reason for this weakness is that we have available a very plausible story about how such things can look designed although they are accidental. This story is the story of Darwinism. So we want to see if we can find *non*living things that looked as though they were designed. Remember, also, that we want nonliving things that were not designed by human beings. It is not so startling to show that a designer exists if the designer turns out to be an engineer at Chrysler. Are there any of the kinds of things for which we are looking?

Actually there is such a thing, but the story about how it shows apparent design is very complicated. In fact, I can only take the word of the physicists that the story goes the way they think it goes. Physicists and cosmologists (scientists who study the beginning of the universe) have recently discovered that it is extremely improbable that *our* universe would come into existence. Lots of the conditions right around the time of the big bang had to be delicately balanced in order to get a universe that could have even simple elements such as carbon or oxygen. Many of these conditions can be described by mathematical equations that have various *constants* in them. A constant is a number in an equation that has a constant value. Other numbers may vary but the constant does not. For example, the area of a circle is πr^2. The value for r (the radius) varies with the size of the circle. Some circles have a radius of 1 centimeter and others have a radius of 12 feet. In either case, the area of these circles can be calculated by squaring the radius and multiplying it by the number π (pronounced "pie"). The number π is 3.14159 (approximately). The number π has this value whenever it is used. Its value is *constant*. That is why it is called a constant. In the same way, equations describing the conditions that were necessary to have a stable universe emerge have constants in them.

Apparently, there are a great many different and seemingly independent equations describing various laws and conditions at the beginning of the universe. Many of these have constants that are such that their values have to be specified quite precisely. For example, if the value of one of the constants was only slightly different, the universe would have expanded so quickly that stars would not have formed and heavy elements would never be synthesized. If the value varied slightly in the other direction, the universe would have collapsed in the first few seconds, thus ruling out the existence of planets, ice cream and polar bears.

I do not know much about the actual equations, but I can tell you it has become very well established that there are many of these equations and that the values have to be set with utmost precision to get a universe with anything interesting in it. Some scientists and philosophers have argued that the odds against the universe's having all of the values set in such a precise way that the universe would be able to sustain life are astronomically great. They resemble the odds of one's going blindfolded into a field that is a square mile in area and picking up the precise blade of grass that had been painted red. Those odds are not good gambling odds. Many people think, as a result, that it is impossible for our universe to have come into being by chance. It had to have been designed.

Rather than pointing to the eye or the brain or a frog, this argument points to the universe itself (given the conditions necessary for its coming into existence) as being the thing that bears the marks of design. The question remains as to whether there is a story—that is, a *plausible* story—that can explain the appearance of design without having to admit that it was, in fact, designed. Some stories have been proposed. We will have to decide whether or not they are plausible. We will discuss briefly the first story in this chapter. In the next chapter, we will look in more detail at what I think is the best story going.

The first story is actually no story at all. Some people have responded by shrugging their shoulders and saying, "We sure are lucky." They reason that the constants in the equations all had to have some value or other and that each particular set of values is as unlikely as any other. The fact that we got dealt a good hand is no more unlikely than our getting dealt any other particular bad hand. If the universe had collapsed nearly instantly, no one would be around to worry about an explanation for why it turned out that way.

Of course, those who respond in this way are correct that every particular setting is equally unlikely no matter what kind of universe results from it. There is still something strange, I think, about the idea that we got one of the few possible universes that can sustain life or even sustain stable physical systems and that it was all simply a lucky chance. I want to try to take this hunch and make it more precise or more persuasive.

One way that some philosophers who write about this issue try to make this hunch more precise is to draw various analogies with other chance situations such as poker games and lotteries. Suppose there was a lottery and you held the only ticket. You were the only player. The lottery was for a billion dollars and your odds of winning were one in a trillion. You randomly picked a number between one and a trillion. As soon as you turn your number into the official, he consults his secret book, turns to you and says, "That is exactly the right number. You have won!" After fainting from shock, I think you will begin to suspect that the lottery was not random at all. You will suspect that the official fixed it in your favor. One way to push this hunch is to ask whether it is more reasonable to believe that you got lucky or that it was fixed in your favor. Not many in this situation will think it is more reasonable to think it was random. The odds against your winning if it is random are just too great.

If this kind of story is a good analogy for the emergence of the universe, then it is not reasonable to think that it was all chance and we got lucky. Of course, it may be that this analogy is not a very good analogy. For example, we know that people sometimes cheat. The hypothesis that the official cheated is not wildly implausible. There is nothing corresponding to our knowledge that people sometimes cheat in the case of the universe. We cannot say that universes sometimes are designed because that is the very idea we are trying to investigate.

Let us look at this case from another angle. While it is not wildly implausible that the official cheated, we really want to ask a different question. Is it at all reasonable to think that the official did not cheat? Given the extreme odds against your winning and the plausibility of his cheating, can you think that you might believe that it was just random? I think the odds are too great. I do not think anyone would conclude it was random, no matter how convincing the official's denial of cheating is. Even if it is impossible to discover how he cheated, it will be more reasonable to think that he did cheat somehow than that the drawing was random. I think looking at this angle can help us see that the idea that the universe emerged as a one-in-a-trillion shot, purely by luck, is not very reasonable. The "no answer" answer is not one to commend itself.

We can adjust the lottery example to make it seem reasonable that you won randomly even if you had a one-in-a-trillion chance of winning. Similarly, we can put forward a story about the emergence of the universe that will be analogous to the adjusted lottery story. This new story about the universe might be enough to undermine the strength of the argument. We will look and see in the next chapter.

13

LOOKING AT THE DETAILS

MANY WORLDS AND SMALL CHANCES

In the last chapter we discussed a lottery example in which you have the only ticket. There is a one-in-a-trillion chance that you will win and yet you do. We thought that it was much more reasonable to suppose that someone cheated than that it was a fair lottery. We can adjust this story a bit and make it seem much less likely that someone cheated. Suppose you enter the lottery with a one-in-a-trillion chance that you win and you do win. Suppose that you know that a trillion tickets were sold—each with a different number. In this case, you will not suspect cheating. (At least you will not suspect cheating if the local lottery officials are not your relatives.)

The moral of this story is that there is nothing unreasonable about thinking that a very unlikely event happens by chance. What makes it reasonable to think you won the lottery by chance is that you know that most of the people lost the lottery. Someone had to win, after all. Stop and think about this last sentence. In a lottery (like the one we are discussing), someone has to win. What is unlikely is that *you* will be the person to win. There is nothing strange about the fact that someone wins. In fact we would expect that someone will win.

Can we carry this lottery story (which is like the actual lotteries that you secretly—you might as well admit it—fantasize about winning) into the discussion of the emergence of the universe? What if our universe is the lucky one that got the constants right to allow it to thrive, but a trillion or more other universes failed to survive? In other words, what if ours is not the only universe? Suppose that there are or have been trillions of different universes, that each is generated by the same processes that can be described by all those mathematical equations and that the values of the constants in those equations are randomly set. In this case, it is not surprising that one of the universes is such that it can sustain life. In fact, we would expect that eventually one would pop out that can do so.

This story does make it reasonable to think that our universe could have arisen by chance. That is, if this story is plausible, it may be reasonable that the universe came into existence by chance rather than by design. If a trillion universes emerge and the values for the mathematical constants are set randomly, sooner or later (probably later) one will emerge that can sustain life and thinking beings and philosophers to ask the questions. While we might still be surprised that we are lucky enough to be in the winning universe, it is no longer surprising that there is some universe or another that has the properties necessary to sustain life.

The idea that many, many universes have emerged with different characteristics is called the *many worlds hypothesis* or the *many worlds conjecture*. I like the name *many worlds conjecture* because it is not really a hypothesis. This conjecture is a story about how the universe can have the marks of apparent design without actually having been designed. It looks as though it could not have come into existence by chance, but appearances are deceiving. It is reasonable, so the conjecture claims, that the whole thing is an accident after all. We do, then, have a story to tell about how what looks designed is not really designed. If this story is true or even plausible, then the design argument concerning the nature of the universe has been strongly undermined.

Is the many worlds conjecture plausible? Well, I want to raise a few doubts about it. First of all, although it sounds like it is a scientific theory, I do not think it is one. This is why I prefer to call it a conjecture rather than a hypothesis. To call it a hypothesis makes it sound scientific; and if it sounds scientific, many people will be inclined to think it is true. It is not quite scientific and, though it may be true, we should not think it is true because we think it is scientific.

Now why do I claim that the many worlds conjecture is not scientific? The reason is this. The many worlds conjecture claims that lots of universes actually exist (or did once exist). The problem is that these other universes, if they exist, are completely inaccessible to us. None of our scientific ways of investigating things can reach them. There is no causal relation between those universes and our own. Causation does not go across universes. Since science explains things largely in terms of causal relations and laws, there can be no scientific *theory* about those universes. All we can have is conjecture about them. It is not that there could not be a science *of* one of these universes. If one exists and it has stable laws of nature, then these laws could be investigated and codified by someone in that universe. This science, however, would not necessarily coincide with our science. Many of the laws would be inconsistent with the laws of nature in our universe. So the conjecture is not quite scientific in the way that we normally understand what it takes for something to be scientific.

I have another related concern about the many worlds conjecture. The many worlds are given as an explanation for our universe instead of a supernatural explanation—God. These universes, I will argue, are themselves (in some sense) supernatural. It might be more accurate to say that these universes are *nonnatural* rather than that they are supernatural. The term *supernatural* often carries the implication of a supernatural *person* such as God or angels. The many worlds conjecture does not explain our universe by appeal to a supernatural person, but I think the explanation is nonnatural nonetheless. So by adopting the many worlds conjecture, we are trading one sort of nonnatural explanation for another.

Why do I think the many universes are nonnatural? Of course, what we will count as natural or as supernatural depends on how we draw the boundaries between the natural and the supernatural. I do not want to fight too hard over these boundaries. I ought to note, though, that many philosophical dictionaries and reference books limit the natural world and natural explanations to those within our universe. I looked up about a dozen definitions in various reference books, and this was the case in almost all of them. Let me give you one example. In the article "Naturalism" in *The Oxford Dictionary of Philosophy,* Simon Blackburn began his explanation of what naturalism is in the following way: "Most generally, a sympathy with the view that ultimately nothing resists explanation by the methods characteristic of the natural sciences."

So naturalism is the view that everything can be explained by the methods of the natural sciences. Something, then, is a *natural* thing if it can be so explained. Notice that the many worlds conjecture is an explanation that appeals to things outside our physical space-time universe. It might be that these things themselves are spatial and temporal and physical, but they are not in *our* space-time universe. Whatever methods of science there are (and it may be that the concept of "methods of science" is very loose in reality), there does not seem to be strong reason to think that these methods will apply to the various universes with all of their differences regarding physical laws and the nature of matter. The methods of science, as we have them, cannot really explain the many worlds. So the many worlds conjecture is not quite a *naturalistic* alternative to God's existence.

If I am right about the many universes being nonnatural, then the design argument we are considering is quite significant. It shows (basically) that either a designer exists or there exist many universes which are outside the domain of science and which are nonnatural things. In either case, naturalism is not a tenable position. Now I think that a view like naturalism is actually more pliable than my first interpretation of Blackburn's definition might imply. (This shows, perhaps, the limits of the use of definitions.) What counts as the criterion for determining what is natural and what is not is something that will change over time. An analogous case is true for what counts as scientific. As new discoveries are added, the boundaries of what counts as scientific are expanded. It is possible that the methods of science will expand in such a way as to include the many universes in their domain. I am skeptical about this possibility, however. Unless we can know something about the nature of these universes, the actual methods we use in science cannot be adapted to accommodate them.

If the many worlds conjecture is plausible, then our new design argument is weakened considerably. If it is possible but we have only very weak reasons for thinking it to be true, then our argument is still pretty strong, though not conclusive. Just as in chapter eight, we have reached the point where it is difficult not to beg the question. And again, I think it helps if we try to assume that it is possible that God exists and to assume that it is possible that God does not exist. If we do not assume that it is possible that God exists, then it seems like the many universe conjecture is the best explanation going for why our universe bears the marks of apparent design. If we do not assume that it is possible that God does *not* exist, then there would be little reason to entertain the many universe conjecture.

I think that the many worlds conjecture might be true. I do not think we can prove that it is false. I also think that we have only weak reasons for thinking it to be true. In fact, without some kind of presumption that no supernatural explanation for the universe is acceptable, I see little evidence in its favor. New evidence may be forthcoming, and if it turns up, it will have to be evaluated accordingly.

It looks like the best story offered to show how the universe has the marks of design without its having been actually designed is not very strong. As a result, this story does not overthrow or substantially weaken the design argument. The argument, though, is not as strong as it would be if no story at all could be offered, but I think the story is too weak to count very much against the argument.

Given the state of the discussion to this point, I think our new design argument provides some reason in favor of thinking that a designer who is not a human being *probably* exists. If I am right, then the last few chapters have given us pretty good reason to think that both the existence of the universe and its nature provide reasons to think God exists. In the next two chapters I want to "look in the mirror." That is, I want to look at some things about human nature that I think also point to the existence of God. I will look specifically at moral reality and at what it implies about there being a purpose for our lives.

14

LOOKING IN THE MIRROR

MORAL REALITY

We began this section on reasons to believe in God by "starting at the beginning." That is, we thought about whether the universe as a whole was caused to begin to exist by something outside of it. Next we "looked at the details" to see if other facts about the universe pointed to the existence of a designer. Now we will "look in the mirror" and consider something more closely related to human nature that may provide reason to believe in God. This thing is moral reality.

Before entering the discussion about moral reality, I must make a couple of things quite clear. First, I am not discussing the idea that one must believe in God in order to be a moral person. I do not think that this idea is true. Nor am I discussing whether those who believe in God are more moral than those who do not. It might be the case that moral reality does point to God even if nonbelievers are more moral than believers. Suppose that you and I have different theories about the nature of numbers. Suppose my theory is right and yours is mistaken. It still might be the case that you are better at doing sums than I am. In the same way, it might be the case that the reality of morality in some way depends on the existence or nature of God while those who practice morality best are not believers in God. The two issues are separate.

The other point I must make clear is that I am also not investigating whether our *knowledge* of morality depends on God. In other words, I do not think that we must believe in God in order to know what is right and what is wrong. If God exists and if he created people, he might have given us a moral sense or intuition by which we can discern to some degree what is right and what is wrong. This sense might be independent of our believing in God. Our sense of smell is independent in this way. God designed it (if he exists), and yet having a discerning sense of smell is not something that belief in God generally improves.

I have to make these points clear because once we begin to talk about morality, things sometimes get a little personal. I am trying to keep the discussion from moving in that direction. If we can keep these issues separate, we can, perhaps, make some progress. What we are interested in, then, is not how we know what is right and wrong, or whether or not we do what we ought to do. We are interested in the nature of morality. What sort of thing is it?

Suppose we begin by taking a look at two everyday sentences:

1. Some geckos eat crickets.

2. It is wrong to torture a cat to death just for fun.

I think that both of these sentences are true. I know the first is true because my family gave me a New Caledonian Crested Gecko for my birthday. I named her Frege after Gottlob Frege, the German philosopher who invented modern symbolic logic. We feed Frege crickets as well as baby food and yogurt. The other day we saw her eat one of the crickets. So we *know* that the sentence "Some Geckos eat crickets" is true.

What is it for a sentence to be true? Without getting into all of the complicated issues about the nature of truth, we can say that a sentence (which is a piece of language) is true if what it says is the case is the case. There is a way things are, and a sentence is true if the way it says things are is the way they are. We can go a little further and say that a sentence is true if it corresponds to or accurately represents a *fact*. For my purposes, I take it that a fact is a piece of the world or part of how the world is. So the fact consisting in my coffee cup's being full of coffee is that part of the world that includes those things. If a piece of language matches a piece of the world in the right way, it is true. This idea of correspondence has fallen into disrepute among some philosophers lately, but I think we can hold to it, at least for now. True sentences have *truth-makers*. Truth-makers are what make true sentences true. So facts are truth-makers of true sentences. In my example about geckos, what makes sentence one true is the fact that Frege eats crickets on occasion. (Of course, I mean the lizard—not the logician. I have no idea what Frege the logician ate.)

Let us think about sentence two for a minute. I think it is true. In fact, I am *certain* that it is true. I am more certain that it is true than I am certain that many other claims are true. What is it, however, that makes it true? You might answer that what makes the sentence true is the *fact that it is wrong to torture a cat to death just for fun*. Fine. What sort of fact is that? Let's call this kind of fact a *moral fact*. In what way is a moral fact a chunk of the world? There are at least three differences between this sort of fact and the fact that renders sentence one true.

First, a moral fact includes moral properties (such as rightness or wrongness), and moral properties are not the kinds of properties that can be observed. We cannot stare at someone torturing a cat and *see* the moral wrongness of the act in the same way that we can watch the lizard eat the cricket. There are, to be sure, other kinds of facts that are unobservable in this way. For example, logical and mathematical facts are not exactly observable, though some of their applications can be observed. The fact that it is impossible for a figure to be both a square and a circle at the same time is a logical fact. The impossibility can be understood but it cannot be observed directly.

The second difference is that if the world were such that there have never been nor ever would be any gecko that ever ate a cricket, it would not be the case that some geckos eat crickets. The lizard fact would not be a fact at all, and the lizard sentence would not be true. If the world were such that no one ever tortured a cat to death just for fun, it would still be the case that it is wrong to torture a cat in this way. The moral fact would still be a fact even though there were actually no actions of the type in question. You see, a moral fact holds whether anyone fulfills the claim that is included in the fact or not. This oddness is also shared by logical and mathematical facts. If there were no triangularly shaped objects, it would still be true that the interior angles of a Euclidean triangle add up to 180 degrees.

The third difference is not, I think, shared with logical and mathematical facts. The fact which makes sentence one true is a fact about the way a chunk of the world *is*. The chunk of the world in question includes lizards and their diets. The sentence about torturing cats is about a different kind of fact: the fact that the action of torturing the poor animal is morally wrong. The truth-maker of sentence two—the moral fact—is not a fact about the way a chunk of the world *is* or, at least, it does not seem to be about the way the world is. It is about the way the world *ought to be*. A moral fact carries with it an obligation on the part of any to whom the fact applies. Philosophers call this feature of moral facts their *normativity*. Moral facts are normative. They tell us what we ought to do. Since *normativity* is not quite descriptive, let's coin our own term for this aspect of moral facts. We can say that they are about *oughtness*. I am not sure *oughtness* is a real word, but it will serve our purposes well. Thinking about the reality of moral facts, then, involves our thinking about oughtness.

So moral facts are a bit strange. They are not your run-of-the-mill sort of facts. This strangeness has led people to worry about moral facts over the years. Some philosophers and many others in our culture have doubted whether there are any moral facts at all. So for the rest of this chapter, I want to discuss several views. These views either deny that there are moral facts or construe moral facts in such a way that it is clear that they do not point to God. I will argue that each of these views is inadequate. In the next chapter I will argue that the existence of moral facts does, indeed, point to God. In other words, moral facts make the existence of God more likely than it would be if there were no moral facts.

Why do many people worry about the nature of moral facts? Really, there are two main reasons. The first is the one I have already mentioned. It is the oddness of moral facts. The second reason that some people worry about the nature of moral facts is that people seem to disagree a lot about what the moral facts are. If there were real truths out there, they might think, we would expect to agree about them. At least we would expect that there would be lots of agreement about them. People and cultures, however, seem to disagree about what is morally acceptable and what is not. This disagreement sheds doubt on the idea that there are facts about morality.

If we conclude that there are no moral facts, as many people do, we need some explanation for why lots of people think that there are moral facts. What is going on when we say things like, "Hey, put that cat down! Don't you know that it is wrong to torture a cat just for fun?" In other words, what explanation can we give for our feeling of morality if we insist on denying moral facts?

The first kind of theory I want to discuss holds that there are no moral facts. This theory simply denies them altogether. This is called *error theory* by some philosophers. Claims such as "It is wrong to torture a cat to death just for fun" do not say anything about any facts. Rather they claim something is a fact when it is not. As a result, claims such as this one are false. It is not wrong to torture a cat to death. The reason it is not wrong is not that it is morally *permissible* to torture cats but that there really is no such thing as moral wrongness (or moral permissibility) at all. If there is no such thing as moral wrongness, then no action can be morally wrong. Hence every claim that some action is wrong or permissible or obligatory turns out to be false.

There have been some very important philosophers who have held this sort of view. Not too many people want to go this way, however. I think that most people want to say that there is at least *something* true about the sentence "It is wrong to torture a cat to death just for fun." It does not seem to be the sort of claim that simply is false. It is true at least in some sense.

The next theory can be called *individual relativism*. Individual relativism is the view that what is morally wrong or morally permissible depends on the opinion of each individual. So each *individual* determines morality. We hear this view a lot when people say things like, "Such and such may be wrong for you but it is OK for me." What is right and wrong varies with the individual and is simply a matter of the individual's opinion.

Notice that I mention two parts to this view here. First, some action may be an obligation for one person, but the same action might be an option for someone else. The second part is that what makes an action an obligation or an option is the individual's opinion about the action. If I think it is wrong to torture cats just for fun, then it is wrong—at least it is wrong for me. If I do not think it is wrong, then it is not. It is important to include both of these parts to individual relativism because on most theories, there are some actions that are obligations for some people but options for others. For example, I have the obligation to make sure my kids have a sufficient education. You do not have that same obligation to my kids. You do have that obligation to your *own* children, if and when you have any. The moral fact in question is the general fact that "parents have obligations to care for their children." Acknowledging that some of our obligations vary in their particular applications is not the same as embracing individual relativism. We also must insist on the second part of the view: what makes something wrong for me is that I think it is wrong.

Although you might be tempted to think that individual relativism denies moral facts, I do not think that it does. One who holds individual relativism might well admit that the sentence "It is wrong to torture a cat to death just for fun" is true. What makes it true, however, is the opinion of the one considering the act. The same act, then, can be morally permissible for me and morally wrong for you. What makes torturing the cat morally wrong for you is a fact. It is the fact that you disapprove of the action. So in one sense, individual relativism does hold that there are moral facts. These facts are individual in that what is a fact as far as one person is concerned is not a fact as far as another is concerned, and both people can be correct in their assessment.

If individual relativism explains moral facts, then these facts do not seem to point to God. There is no need for some person or purpose or standard beyond human beings because it is the individual human being who determines what is morally correct. Each human person and her opinions provide all of the authority or grounding that we can want as far as moral claims are concerned. There is no need for God in our moral theory.

Why might someone think that individual relativism is the truth about morals? I think people are tempted to hold this view when they face the fact that many people disagree about moral issues. Almost any moral question admits of various answers, and there are many people who hold to these various answers. I also think that people do not want other people to tell them what to do and that people do not want to tell others what to do. If morals are individually relative, then no one can *tell* you that something is wrong. Your beliefs determine that the action is wrong. Your opinions of the matter make it so.

I think that individual relativism is not a very good position. Furthermore, I think that most people will not continue to hold it when they are challenged with its implications. The problem with this kind of relativism is what we can call the *schoolyard bully problem*. For example, if the individual determines morality, and if I believe it is morally permissible for me to steal your stereo, then it is permissible for me to do it. I don't think that many people really think that it is OK to steal from someone (at least, if you do not need to steal to save someone's life). If we want to hold that morality boils down to individual relativism, we have to let bullies be bullies. We cannot hold that it is wrong for them to bully other people.

The third position looks like it can solve the schoolyard bully problem. We can call this view *cultural relativism*. On this view, it is not each individual who determines her own morality. What is right or wrong is determined by one's culture or society. Even if the bully thinks it is morally fine for him to bully someone, our culture says that it is not fine. Therefore, it is wrong for the bully to act in this way. Some people like cultural relativism because they see that different cultures (either different cultures today or different cultures throughout history) have different ideas about what is right and what is wrong.

I think it is clearer that cultural relativism acknowledges the reality of moral facts. These facts also do not point to anything outside human culture. As a result, they do not point to God. God is not needed in this moral theory either.

I do not think that cultural relativism is a very good position. We still have a bully problem. The problem is not a *schoolyard* bully (usually just one big guy who is followed around by his less-than-intelligent gang), it is a *cultural* bully. Let's face it, some cultures push other cultures around. This is why there is racism and war. If I live in a completely racist society, would racism be right for me? According to cultural relativism, the answer is yes, it would be. Furthermore, it may be that in my culture, racism is not just permitted, but it is commanded. If it is commanded in my culture, then I am obligated to be a racist. In other words, it may be that it would be morally wrong for me not to be a racist. Well, this position no longer sounds very plausible.

One other problem with cultural relativism is the *hero problem*. All of our greatest heroes (apart from sports heroes, actors and rock stars) have been men and women who have stood up and called their own society wrong. If culture is what determines morality, it is always morally wrong to criticize society. Are all of our heroes wrong? I do not think so. I think they were right. People like Martin Luther King Jr. claimed that their own culture was severely mistaken about certain moral issues. Any culture that said that racial segregation was perfectly fine was actually morally wrong. The reason Dr. King is a hero is that he criticized his own society. If moral facts are made up by each culture, then he was deeply mistaken. Not only was he deeply mistaken, but he was grossly immoral because he led tens of thousands of other people astray.

Relativism, whether individual or cultural, has some serious problems. Now to reject relativism is not to claim that it is easy to figure out what is right and what is wrong. In many cases, there are deep disagreements and it is difficult to sort them out. This difficulty, though, is not a reason to hold to relativism.

Relativism continues to be very popular and is the main kind of moral idea that you will see on television. Because we are learning to think through these kinds of questions, we are less likely simply to absorb the kind of moral thinking that you see on a talk show or a sitcom. Relativism, though, is not the only kind of theory that claims that morality does not need a divine explanation. The fourth theory is, I think, much more interesting and more persuasive to good thinkers.

We can call the fourth theory the *evolutionary theory of morality.* Some people claim that the reason human beings have such a deep sense of morality is that it helped the human race survive. A long time ago, some individual people began to live and work together for mutual protection. These groups became communities that shared in the hunting and gathering and maybe in the raising of children and the defending of the group against enemies. People who were in groups like this survived better than did those who never joined in a group. Along the way, people developed a loyalty to their group, and they felt guilty if they did not contribute or do their share in protecting the group. This loyalty and guilt and other related feelings developed eventually into our conscience, or moral sense. We have a moral sense, then, because we inherited it from our prehistoric ancestors along with opposable thumbs and the ability to walk erect and to get acne. Morality has survival value.

Before I tell you why I do not believe this theory in the least, I have to say that none of my reasons for rejecting the evolutionary theory of morality have to do with the biological theory of evolution. You see, this theory of morality is not a biological theory. It takes its *name* from a very important biological theory. The moral theory itself is not scientific at all. It is simply a speculation about what might have happened.

Why do I think the evolutionary theory of morality is not a good explanation for moral facts? First of all, it is not an explanation of moral facts at all. A moral fact is something like, "It is wrong to torture a cat to death just for fun." What the evolutionary theory of morality does explain (that is, if it is true) is why we may *feel* like it is wrong to torture a cat just for fun. It explains moral *feelings,* but it cannot explain moral *facts.* Even if we did learn our moral feelings the way the evolutionary theory says that we did, the fact that it is wrong to torture the cat is a fact that is both odd (in the ways we discussed at the beginning of this chapter) and unexplained. Explaining why we *think* that torturing the feline is wrong does not explain the fact that it is wrong.

Some people do think that if we explain the moral feeling, we explain away the moral fact. In other words, they think that moral facts reduce to moral feelings. There are no moral facts. There is nothing to morality beyond our feelings. As we said earlier, it is a legitimate philosophical move to defend an error theory. The evolutionary theory of morality, however, does not itself *defend* the claim that moral feelings are the entire story of morality. It does not even attempt to do so. It simply assumes it.

I suppose if you thought, for some reason, that everything in the world *must* be explained with some kind of evolutionary theory, then this account might appeal to you. But why would anyone think that *morality* must be explained by a *biological* theory? Some of the people who hold this theory do so because they are committed to explaining morality *by evolution*. If you are simply trying to explain morality—by whatever means—you have better explanations from which to choose.

So my first reason to reject the evolutionary theory of morality is that it does not explain morality. That an explanation fails to explain is generally a good reason to look elsewhere. The second reason I reject this theory is that there is no evidence that it is true. We may have evidence that prehistoric people did travel and hunt in groups, but we do not have (and we cannot have) any evidence that our sense of moral obligation comes from the feelings of loyalty and guilt and so forth. This claim is not the sort of claim that lends itself to physical evidence.

The third problem with this theory is related to the first one. Evolutionary theory, as far as biology is concerned, is an explanation about how species vary and develop through random variation and natural selection. The key is natural selection. Individuals that are not well suited do not, for the most part, survive. The species survives because the better-adapted individuals have the most surviving offspring. They pass on their better traits to their offspring and so the species survives. If our moral sense originated because it had survival value, how should we think *now* about these moral feelings? We should think that they *were* biologically useful. What we should not think is that they tell us anything that is true. Although we may continue to feel as though we have a real obligation to act in a certain way, if this theory is true, we know that we do not have any real obligations. These moral feelings, though they had survival value in the past, now are like one's appendix. They are leftovers that have outlived their purpose. It is hard to see what the purpose for moral feelings would be now.

We have covered a lot of ground in this chapter. First we looked at what kind of fact a moral fact is. Next we pointed out that many people want to say there are no moral facts or that moral facts can be explained without appealing to anything beyond human culture. We looked at four different approaches to the nature of morality. Although we really only glanced at them, I think we have seen enough to reject them. It seems as though there are good reasons to think that there are moral facts and that these facts are not explained easily. What these facts have to do with God is the topic of the next chapter.

15

LOOKING IN THE MIRROR

MORAL FACTS POINT TO GOD

In the last chapter we looked at the nature of moral facts. We saw that they are odd in various ways. We also looked at two different kinds of relativism and concluded that each of these should be rejected. We then investigated the evolutionary theory of morality, and I concluded that it, too, comes up short as an explanation for morality.

In this chapter, I will argue that the existence of moral facts points to the existence of God. I do not think that I am giving a tight argument or proof that the existence of moral facts shows that there is a God. Rather, I am going to press the idea that the existence of a God who created us and cares about us is the *best explanation* for the existence of moral facts. Of course what counts as the best explanation depends on what all of the alternative explanations are. I am not going to check out every possible explanation. Rather I am going to compare the idea that God exists with the idea that God does not exist. These are the two major competing explanations. Actually the claim that God exists and the claim that God does not exist are not, by themselves, explanations at all. The claim that God exists may provide the *resources* for some explanations. These explanations will rely on particular ideas about the nature or purposes of God. The claim that there is no God is a position that *rules out* certain explanations. That is, it rules out explanations that appeal to the nature or purposes of God. There are many different and incompatible explanations that fit into the "no God" side of the fence. So, to be precise, I will argue that God's existence provides better resources for an ex-

planation for moral facts than the idea that the universe and everything in it is the product of purposeless processes.

Starting from the assumption that there are moral facts, we can get
to the hunch I am pressing rather quickly. One of the things that
makes moral facts strange is their *oughtness*. So we need to look into
oughtness. We should begin by observing that there are areas of life
other than the moral area that also exhibit oughtness. Activities such
as playing a game and doing homework involve oughtness.

Think of the game of chess. There are two different ways oughtness applies to chess. The first involves the simple rules of the game.
You are allowed to move your bishop only on the diagonal. If you
move your bishop across the horizontal, you break the rules and, in
some sense, you are no longer playing chess. The other sense of
oughtness is a strategic oughtness. You ought to protect your king. If
you do not protect your king adequately, you will lose. You will not
be violating any rules. As far as the rules are concerned, you will be
playing fine. You might not be a very good player, though. The
oughtness that applies to doing your homework is largely a strategic
oughtness. If you do not do your homework, you will not do well in
school. If you do not do well in school, your future options will most
likely be more limited than you want them to be.

If you challenge one of the rules in game playing, there are two
different replies. These replies correspond to the type of oughtness
being challenged. If it is a strategic rule you challenge, the response
will be a prudential one. If I tell you that you must protect your king
and you question me, I will appeal to your goal of winning (or, at
least, of not losing so quickly that it is embarrassing). If you try to
violate a fundamental rule of chess, such as moving your bishop
along the horizontal, I will say, "You can't do that." If you challenge
me, I will appeal to the rules. If you say, "Why should I follow the
rules?" then my only response is that if you don't, you are no longer
playing chess. So *if* you want to play chess, you have to follow the
rules. If you ask me why you should do your homework, I will also
give you a prudential reply, such as, "You will not do well on the test
if you do not prepare."

So we can see that playing chess and doing homework are *arenas of oughtness*. (Isn't that a cool phrase?) What clues do these arenas of oughtness give us about the nature of moral facts? In game playing, you have to act in a certain way. There are rules that govern your behavior, and you must follow them. As far as homework is concerned, there are things you must do. In this way, these arenas are similar to the moral area of our lives. We are under real obligations to act in certain ways.

In the case of chess, you are free to reject the rules of the game. The consequence is that you are no longer playing chess. In school, you can decide that you do not care to do very well. In both cases, you avoid the oughtness. Some philosophers have called obligations like these *hypothetical imperatives*. They are imperatives because they are rules or commands. They are, however, only hypothetical. That is, they are binding only in particular circumstances. The circumstances in which you are bound by hypothetical imperatives are those in which you have a certain desire and that desire requires that you follow the rule. We could also call them *conditional commands*. They are commands, but they are only conditional commands. If you do not want to fulfill the condition, then you do not have to fulfill the command. *If* you want to play chess correctly, you must follow the rule about not moving your bishop across the horizontal. *If* you want to get into college or get a good job, you have to pass math. *If* you want to pass math, you have to do your homework. Are moral facts also hypothetical imperatives? Are they conditional? Let us think about these questions.

Suppose you accuse one of your friends of doing something morally wrong. What kind of response will you get from her? I think you are likely to get a couple of kinds of responses. First, she may argue with you that she did not do the morally wrong action. It was not a lie after all because she was truly mistaken. In order for it to count as a lie, she must have deceived you intentionally. Or she may argue that she did it but that she had a good reason to do it. Yes, it was a lie, but if she did not lie, then your other friend's feelings would have been hurt. In other words, there are special circumstances which apply that make the lie something that is not morally wrong. What you are not likely to hear her say is something like the following: "Yes, I lied but so what? I do not want to be moral anyway." Now you *might* get this sort of response, but I think it is not likely. Most of us think that we do not have a choice about whether we are going to "play the morality game" like we do with the homework strategy or a chess game. We are stuck with the morality game. We cannot opt out.

One major difference between conditional imperatives and morality lies precisely at this point. If you decide not to play chess, then the rules do not apply to you. You are under no obligation to keep them. If you decide that you do not want to do well in school, then the obligation you would otherwise feel to do your homework is undermined. Whether or not moral rules apply to you, however, is not up to you. Deciding that you do not want to be a moral person does not get you out of the moral obligation. If you cannot opt out of the morality game, then morality is not about hypothetical imperatives. It is not conditional. Morality consists in what philosophers call *categorical imperatives*. We could call them *unconditional imperatives* or *unconditional commands*. You simply must obey. No one thinks you are excused if you tell them you decided not to obey the dictates of morality.

Two points must be made here. First, if there are no moral facts, or if morality is relative in the way we discussed in the last chapter, then this claim about the unconditional nature of morality is not true. If we can reject relativism, as I argued, and if there are moral facts, then it is reasonable to think that moral obligations are unconditional imperatives. If they are not conditional, then you cannot opt out.

Second, it is certainly up to the individual whether she will care about acting morally or not. Even if there are moral facts and these are unconditional, she can decide that she will not try to act morally. Her decision, however, does not remove the real moral obligations that she has. She still did something really wrong, even if she does not care.

So it looks like we have an arena of oughtness that is unconditional. We are not free to reject the condition. The command is binding on us whether or not we want it to be. What is it that makes morality binding on us? It must be something that is not up to us, because if it was up to us, we could, perhaps, opt out. I want to pursue one line of thought about this question.

In each hypothetical arena of oughtness, the oughtness is related to a purpose. In chess, the purpose is to play the game or to play it well. In homework, it is to do well enough in your class that you can move on to your next step in life. Moral imperatives—unconditional imperatives—have something to do with purpose as well. At least, this is the claim I want to make. The purpose of an unconditional imperative itself must be unconditional. It must be a purpose that holds for each person regardless of his particular circumstances. It is a purpose that we are not free to reject. If there is such a purpose, it is easy to see how we could be under unconditional imperatives. We are under imperatives because there is a purpose. They are not conditional because this purpose is not something we choose. It is given to us. So my first conclusion is that the nature of morality is good reason to think that there is a purpose for human existence.

I want to pause and make clear the relation between the imperatives and the purpose. It might seem like I am going in two different directions here. It may help to distinguish between the order of *reality* and the order of *knowing*. I can explain this best with an example. If I am going to drive into Boston, I will need a good map. There is a relation between the city of Boston and the map of Boston. The city itself comes first in the order of *reality*. It was there and the streets were arranged in that particular sort of disorder for which Boston is known before the map was made. Later, someone drew up the map to show how the streets of Boston work. It is a good map only if it represents accurately the relevant features of the city of Boston. As far as the order of *knowing* is concerned, the map comes first. I need to study the map in order to get the right clues about navigating the city.

When it comes to purposes and rules, the purpose comes first in the order of reality. The objective of the game of chess determines what the particular rules are. The rules might come first, though, in the order of knowing. I learn chess by learning the different pieces and the moves they are allowed to make. From there I move on to the goal of the game. The same relation holds in the area of morality. In the order of knowing, the existence and nature of moral facts come first. These then give us a clue that there is a purpose and that this purpose is unconditional. In the order of reality, however, the purpose comes first.

Let's get back to the main discussion and try to see in another way how moral facts give a clue to the purpose of morality. Suppose there is no unconditional purpose for human existence. In this case it is difficult to see how there can be categorical imperatives. The question that is lurking here is, Why should I feel like I must obey the moral rules? When we were investigating chess and homework, we saw that any answer to this kind of "why" question will be an answer in terms of purpose. If I can reject any purpose that I consider, then whatever obligation I am under is not unconditional.

Perhaps I should mention that I do not want to argue that some *particular* moral rule is itself absolute and unconditional. I am not saying, for example, that you are never allowed to lie. It may be the case that a lie is never morally justified, or it may be the case that there are circumstances in which you are morally justified to lie. Remember, if you do lie in one of these circumstances, you have not rejected the moral game. You have applied your best thinking and concluded that the unconditional moral obligations you have do not prohibit you from lying in that particular situation. You are clearly still in the moral game. What I am arguing is that your obligation to follow the moral imperatives—whatever these turn out to be—is itself unconditional.

The difference between the purposes of hypothetical imperatives and that of categorical imperatives is that we are free to reject the former but not the latter. We are free to reject the purposes of hypothetical imperatives because they are, in a sense, conditions that were invented by ourselves or by other human beings. Someone invented chess and made up the rule about not moving your bishop across the horizontal. If the purpose that grounds moral obligations is one we cannot reject, it is probably not one that was invented by any human being or group of people. It is not one we choose; it is one that we find that we have whether we like it or not.

So our reasoning to this point can be summarized in this way. Moral facts involve unconditional or categorical imperatives. These imperatives are not invented by people or by society. One very plausible way to understand imperatives is in terms of purpose. Unconditional imperatives require an unconditional purpose. So the nature of morality is good reason to think that there is a purpose for human beings and that this purpose is not invented by people or society, nor is it optional.

The final step in this chapter is to point out that the existence of this kind of purpose for human beings is pretty surprising if there is no God and human beings are, in the end, accidental byproducts of accidental processes. Yet such a purpose is not at all surprising if God exists and created human beings. If God invented human beings, he did so for a reason or reasons. Some of these reasons may ground moral truths. For example, if God made us with moral ends in mind—if he made us so that we would embody certain virtues, for example—his setting up moral reality the way he did makes a good deal of sense. If God has spiritual purposes for us—that we would find a relationship with him and experience him as our highest good—he may set up moral rules as guidelines for how best to do that.

Whatever God's purposes are, it makes sense that he would make us the kinds of beings that are subject to moral truths and that can understand and act on them. If God's purposes are for our good, as many religious traditions affirm, then the fact that following moral reality tends toward our flourishing also makes sense. God's existence, then, is a better explanation for the nature of morality than any view that does not include an unconditional purpose. Morality, then, points to God's existence.

16

REASONS TO BELIEVE

THE CUMULATIVE CASE

Suppose someone has died. We are not sure whether the victim died of natural causes or was killed by another person on purpose. A detective examines the scene and begins a long investigation. She aims, first, to find out if the best explanation for the death of the person includes the purposeful actions of another. Her investigation will have the secondary aim of identifying the responsible person, if there is one. She pursues this goal by gathering lots of facts at the scene and determining in which direction these facts point. Some of the lines of evidence will point to the fact that the death was caused by some person, rather than by some accident, without identifying who the person is. Other lines of evidence may go far toward identifying the person, once the detective has concluded that the death was not accidental. Sometimes what first appears to be a promising line of evidence turns out to be a dead end. Other times, some fact that appears to be insignificant winds up providing the key.

It is unusual, I think, for a detective to find a single piece of evidence that will itself provide absolute certainty about the identity of the criminal. Rather, detectives try to build what can be called a *cumulative case* to identify the guilty person. The various lines of evidence work together to make it more and more reasonable to think that there was a murder and that a particular suspect is guilty. If there are enough lines of evidence and the cumulative case is strong enough, the suspect may be convicted of the crime. The evidence needs to establish murderer's identity "beyond a reasonable doubt."

There is a great deal of similarity between the strategy of the detective and the strategy we have been pursuing in our role as philosophers. We do not expect one argument or line of evidence by itself to be strong enough to *prove* that God exists or to make the case *undeniably* strong. Rather, different lines work together to strengthen the case for God's existence. We also do not expect one line of evidence to show that the cause of the universe, for instance, must have all of the attributes that are traditionally associated with God. One line might point to some supernatural cause, while another line might point to the notion that the cause is most likely a person. Together, the various lines make a cumulative case that the universe is caused to be what it is by some being that is significantly like the God of some religious traditions.

In this section we have looked at three lines of evidence. I argued that each of these points to the existence of God. None of them brought certainty or the kind of evidence that would overwhelm someone. I think it is fair to say that each of these lines of evidence, individually, made it somewhat more likely that God exists than that he does not. I argued that the existence of the universe is better explained by a first cause who is a powerful person, outside space and time. I also argued that the nature of the universe is better explained by a cause that was an intelligent designer who had some interest in a universe that was suitable for life. Finally, the nature of moral facts indicate that there is a purpose to our lives that comes from outside human culture. This purpose gives us reason to think that God has an interest in individual persons and that he cares about our flourishing.

These three arguments are not the only lines of evidence there are for God's existence. There are many other lines we could have pursued. I chose to pursue these three arguments because they are among the most popular lines of evidence for God and because they bring up the kind of philosophical issues that are most worth discussing in a book of this kind. There are other lines of evidence that begin from things such as human consciousness, the nature of numbers and even the kind of being God must be if he exists. These arguments are also philosophically fruitful and may further strengthen the case for the existence of God. I do think they are a bit less accessible and therefore less critical to the task of taking our *first steps* in philosophy.

Thinking about the three arguments we discussed as part of a cumulative case strengthens the total case for the existence of God. If each argument gives some reason to think it is a bit more likely that God exists than that he does not, the total effect of the arguments makes this conclusion even more secure. How secure is the conclusion that God exists? I think we have pretty strong evidence but, again, it is not overwhelming evidence.

We must remember that we have only considered reasons *to* believe in God. We have not yet considered reasons to believe there is no God. Reasons to think that God does not exist also belong in the cumulative case. For the detective, some lines of evidence point toward a particular suspect, and some point away from that same person. We need to take all of the lines into consideration and assess the total cumulative case regarding the existence of God. In the next section, we will look in some detail at the best argument against the existence of God.

PART THREE

THE SQUARE CIRCLE OBJECTION

Evil is all-pervasive. Everywhere we go, everywhere we look, we are faced with evil. Not only do we see it with our own eyes as we walk the streets of our city or our campus, but television, radio and the newspapers thrust the reality of evil into our faces every day.

Evil is a problem for thinking people. We want to understand it, explain it and make sense of our lives in light of it. When we step back to take a look at evil, we see that it is very hard to define. So I do not want to try to give a formal definition of evil. I should, however, say something about what I mean when I use the word *evil*. I am taking the term *evil* to cover the whole variety of bad things that happen—everything from the great atrocities, such as AIDS and the Holocaust, to the less cosmic sufferings, such as loneliness. I would count physical pains and relational problems as evil as well. Perhaps we think that things are evil if we have a hunch that they *ought not be that way*.

When a person asks me, "What about God and evil?" I often ask, "What kind of evil do you have in mind?" I ask this question because there are a variety of issues that are raised when thinking about God and evil. I want to know what kind of question the person is asking. I want to know especially if he is thinking of evil in general or if he is dealing with and struggling to understand some particular experience with evil. So I ask, "What kind of evil do you have in mind?" One kind of answer is a bit abstract, such as "You know, war, disease and things like that." Another kind of answer is concrete: "Well, my parents just got divorced." These two answers indicate two very different questions about God and evil.

In the first case, the question about God and evil is usually a philosophical question. Something about evil makes it seem odd to claim that God exists. If God is good, he ought to fix it. Since it is obviously broken, maybe there is no God. We will spend most of our time on this part of the question. In the second case, the question is usually less philosophical and more, for lack of a better word, *existential*. A person who is asking the more existential question is not raising a *theoretical objection* to belief in God. Rather, that person is raising a *difficulty* to belief in God. And it is not a challenge to belief in God in general but a challenge to *his* believing in God in *his* situation. It is not only those who believe in God that may face the existential challenge. Sometimes our experience of evil raises a deep difficulty to our making sense of our lives or our situations. The difficulty is the same whether or not it is connected to questions about God.

Sometimes these questions do overlap. A person who is struggling with evil and suffering may find herself asking the philosophical questions in response. Sometimes, I think, questioning the existence of God may begin because of one's sense of disappointment rather than because of a line of reasoning. Disappointment can bring disillusionment, and disillusionment can get quite a grip on us. It may be the case that, next to the grip of disillusionment, whatever *reasons* we can think of to believe that God exists or that God is good will appear weak. So sometimes the reason we do not believe or the reason we stop believing is not the intellectual challenge to believing in God. Sometimes, the grip of disillusionment cannot be matched by things that seem to be only abstract and theoretical.

So what do we do? Now, you know that I am a philosopher, so you can be pretty sure that I am not going to go on and say that reasons to believe in God are not important. They are important. In fact, I think they are very important. I do not think, however, that they are the whole story. When you and I are suffering from disappointment or from disillusionment, we do not need more reasons to believe in God. At least we do not need more *philosophical* reasons. We need to see the reality of God in the lives of other people. Although we may be asking, why does God let this happen? we might not need to know why at all. We need to know that God is there and that he holds us in his hands. Knowing why he lets something happen, even if we could know why, does not bring assurance of his presence. When my daughter, Elizabeth, skins her knee, she does not need or want a lesson in neurology in order to understand why it hurts. She wants to be held while she hurts. I know I am not very different than my daughter. I need to be held as I go through suffering.

I want to know, when one of my friends asks about evil, if he needs answers or if he needs to sense the comfort of the presence of God. If I get confused on this point and I launch into the philosophical discussion, I will not be giving him what he most needs. He will not in all likelihood sense that God is holding him up through his pain. There is a time to speak, and there is a time to be silent.

In this section of the book we are going to look mostly at the philosophical question. It is not that this is completely irrelevant to sorting out the existential question. If you have a good handle on the philosophical question, you will be less likely to allow disappointment to become disbelief. For many people, the task of reconciling God and evil seems impossible. The philosophical question is a deep and real obstacle to their believing in God. So we will look into what philosophers call *the problem of evil.*

The problem of evil is actually an argument. More precisely, it is a family of arguments. These are arguments from the existence or nature or distribution of evil to the conclusion that God does not or probably does not exist. These arguments have been among the greatest objections to theism, that is, belief in God, since theism has been around. If it is not the greatest philosophical problem with theism, it is at least the problem with the greatest emotional impact. Everywhere and in every age, sensitive thinkers have been confronted with the magnitude of evil in the world and have wondered if God exists after all. The existence of evil is seen as proof or evidence that there is no all-powerful, all-loving God.

As we have seen, many philosophical ideas and arguments begin with a hunch. It just *seems* that something is the case. Building on a hunch, you can try to make arguments or come up with reasons that the hunch is correct. The square circle objection begins with the hunch that there is something strange about the existence of both God and evil. Because God is supposed to be all-powerful and good (and not just pretty good but morally perfect), evil seems out of place in his universe. After all, if *you* were powerful enough, wouldn't you fix lots of the evil in the world? So the hunch is that God and evil are contradictory. In other words, it is impossible that God exists and that evil exists. One of them might exist, but both cannot. Just like in geometry, it is possible that a figure is a square and it is possible that a figure is a circle. What is not possible is for the same figure to be both a square and a circle. Some people have pressed the charge that believing both in God and in evil is like believing in square circles. It is believing in an impossibility. Since it is pretty clear that evil exists, it must be the case that there is no God.

Let us take this hunch and make it more precise. If we can build an argument for the conclusion that God and evil cannot both exist, we will be making progress. Rather than making up my own version of such an argument, I will use one that has become fairly well known, at least as far as anything in philosophy becomes well known.

In 1955 a British philosopher named John Mackie published a paper, "Evil and Omnipotence," in the journal *Mind* on this topic. He claimed that God and evil were incompatible. Mackie paid careful attention to making the hunch precise. Much of the discussion of the problem of evil in recent years has begun with Mackie's paper.

In his paper, Mackie claims that the following two statements are inconsistent. (I am paraphrasing Mackie, here, to make the argument a little bit more clear. Note that Mackie actually left out the phrase *all-knowing* here and below, but I added it to make the argument stronger.)

1. God exists and is wholly good, all-powerful and all-knowing.

2. Evil exists.

If these are logically inconsistent, they cannot both be true. Given that it is obvious that evil exists, God cannot exist. While it may seem as though these are inconsistent, it is not obvious that this is so. How does Mackie make this hunch precise? He says that we can show that these are inconsistent by *deriving a contradiction* from them. He claims that we can derive a contradiction by adding two additional statements to the argument. The statements he adds are the following:

3. There are no limits to what an all-powerful, all-knowing being can do.

4. A good being always prevents evil as far as it can.

These statements, Mackie thinks, are not controversial. He thinks they are just explanations of what it means to say that God is wholly good and all-powerful and all-knowing. If he can derive a contradiction from the things that are supposed to be true of God, he can show successfully that God does not exist. Let us take these four statements and show, step by step, how we can, in fact, derive the contradiction.

First we list the four statements.

1. God exists and is wholly good, all-powerful and all-knowing.

2. Evil exists.

3. There are no limits to what an all-powerful, all-knowing being can do.

4. A good being always prevents evil as far as it can.

From these we can go step by step.

5. *If (1) and (4) are true, then* God prevents all of the evil he can prevent—because he is good.

6. *If (1) and (3) are true, then* God *can* prevent all of the evil there is—because he is powerful and smart enough.

7. *If (5) and (6) are true, then* God prevents all evil.

8. *If (7) is true, then* there is no evil.

9. *If (2) and (8) are true, then* there is evil and there is no evil.

Statement 9 is the contradiction. Mackie claims that this argument shows that either statement 1 or statement 2 is false. It is obvious that statement 2 is true. (There is evil, after all.) So, Mackie concludes, statement 1 is false. There is no God who is wholly good, all-powerful and all-knowing. He thinks he has *proven* that there is no God.

What do we do with Mackie's argument? Has he proven that God does not exist? First, we need to remember what it takes for an argument to be a proof. We discussed this in the beginning of the last section, but I will repeat myself a bit here. There are different types of arguments. The kind we are thinking about is called a *deductive argument*. In order for a deductive argument to be a proof, it has to pass two tests. The first test is whether the conclusion *follows from* the premises. In order to be a proof, an argument must be such that each step leads to the next without any jumps or loopholes. We call a deductive argument that passes this test a *valid argument*. An argument has to be valid if it is to be a proof. Not every valid argument, however, is a proof. In order to be a proof, an argument has to pass the second test as well. The second test for a proof is whether all of the premises are true. If a deductive argument passes both of these tests, it is a proof.

Let us look again at Mackie's argument. Is it a proof? Well, see if it passes both tests. Does the conclusion follow from the premises? Are the premises true? Mackie thought it passed both tests. He thought he had a proof. If he is right, then the existence of both God and evil *is* contradictory. If there is evil, God does not exist. Believing in God, if this is so, is like believing in a square circle. It is believing in something that is not possible.

Before you look at the next chapter, look over the argument carefully. Do you think it does pass both tests? In the next chapter we will look at it together, but before we do, I want you to look at it yourself. Did he jump over any steps? Are all of his premises true? Which steps or premises might you call into question?

18

GOD AND EVIL RECONCILED

In the previous chapter, we looked at the square circle objection. That is, we looked at an argument from evil to the conclusion that God does not exist. If that argument is successful, it is a proof that there is no God. As we said, in order for the argument to be a proof, it must pass two tests. First, the argument has to be valid. That is, the conclusion has to follow from the premises without jumping over any steps or leaving any loopholes. Second, it has to be the case that the premises are true. If both of these tests are passed, the argument is a proof.

Let us look carefully at the argument from the last chapter. Here it is:

1. God exists and is wholly good, all-powerful and all-knowing.

2. Evil exists.

3. There are no limits to what an all-powerful, all-knowing being can do.

4. A good being always prevents evil as far as it can.

5. *If (1) and (4) are true, then* God prevents all of the evil he can prevent—because he is good.

6. *If (1) and (3) are true, then* God *can* prevent all of the evil there is—because he is powerful and smart enough.

7. *If (5) and (6) are true, then* God prevents all evil.

8. *If (7) is true, then* there is no evil.

9. *If (2) and (8) are true, then* there is evil and there is no evil.

Notice, first of all, that the argument *is* valid. Each step follows
from the previous steps. In order to show that this argument is *not* a
proof, then, we must find at least one of its premises to be false. If
they are all true, the argument proves there is no God.

Which premise might we challenge? We might try to deny that evil
exists. I do not think that this is a good move. It is obvious that there
is evil. Furthermore, most theists believe in evil. The major religions
do not make any sense at all if there is no evil. The central point of
many religions, for example, is some kind of redemption from sin. If
there is no evil, there is no need for redemption. So anyone who denies the existence of evil is denying one of the central aspects of theism. So denying evil, although it would defeat the argument, is not a
satisfactory answer for anyone, theist or atheist.

We might hold that either God is not all-powerful, or he is not all-
knowing, or he is not wholly good. In other words, we could deny
the first premise without denying that God exists. We could say that
God exists but that he is limited in power or limited in knowledge
and that he is doing the best he can. We may think that God is all-
powerful and all-knowing but that he does not care as much as we
might have thought.

You might be surprised to find out that many people hold one of
these alternatives. Deists hold that God created the world but lets it
go and does not care much about what happens. Thomas Jefferson
was a famous deist. Other thinkers hold that God is not all-powerful:
he is limited in power and is working out his plan the best he can.
The most popular form of this thinking is called *process theology*. It
became famous in the early part of the twentieth century and is still
widely discussed. Holding either one of these alternatives will allow
you to continue to believe in God in the face of this argument. John
Mackie's argument will not count against either of these views.

I do not think we want to conclude that God either does not care
or is limited in power. For one thing, each of these conclusions denies things that are pretty central to any traditional view of God. The
traditional view is that God is quite concerned with us. Furthermore,
God is thought to be the creator of the universe. If he created the

world, it does not seem that the world can limit God's abilities. I think we do not want to think that premise 2 is the false one. We have to look at the other premises:

3. There are no limits to what an all-powerful, all-knowing being can do.

4. A good being always prevents evil as far as it can.

Are these true? If they are, then the argument proves that there is no God. It turns out that *both* of them are false. Let us take them one at a time, beginning with what it means to say that God is all-powerful.

What does it mean that God is all-powerful? Can he do anything? *Can God make a rock so big that he can't move it?* (What about this one—*can God make a class so boring that even he falls asleep?*) Some people think this question is one of the basically unanswerable questions. I can answer it. In fact the answer is pretty easy. Here it is. *No, he cannot!*

There. That was not too difficult, was it? Wait a minute! If God cannot make this rock, then he is not all-powerful, right? Again, the answer is no. Let me explain. A physical object that is so big that an all-powerful being cannot move it is a contradiction. There cannot be such a thing. It is like a square circle. So God cannot make one. You see, to say that God is all-powerful does not mean that God can do any task I can name in words. It means that he can do anything that is not a logical contradiction. A square circle is a logical contradiction. It is a logical impossibility. It is not a genuine possibility. It is really not a thing at all and therefore it is not surprising that God cannot make one. It is not a real limit to God's power that he cannot perform contradictions.

I know that you might be thinking that this is where I sneak in and set the deck of cards in my favor. Or, to change metaphors, I have put a loophole into the system. Let me assure you that I have not pulled a trick. There are two reasons I can make this claim. First, throughout the history of thinking about God's power, almost no major thinker has held that God can do contradictions. The only possible exceptions are René Descartes and, maybe, Martin Luther. Descartes thought that God could have made different mathematical truths. Second, the claim that God cannot do contradictions is *not* a loophole for the one who believes in God. In fact, it makes our job more difficult. It is the *atheist* who ought to insist that God's being all-powerful does not imply that he can do contradictions. I will explain why. The atheist wants to give an argument that God does not exist. The best kind of argument (like the one we are discussing) tries to show that the existence of God leads to a contradiction. Anything that leads to a contradiction cannot be true. So if the existence of God leads to a contradiction, we know that God does not exist.

But if God can make contradictions true, these kinds of arguments cannot succeed. In fact, no argument against the existence of God can succeed! Let me show you how this works. Let's pretend that the argument from evil we are discussing is a successful proof that God does not exist. We show that if evil exists, then it is impossible that God exists. All the believer has to say in response is, "So what? Why should I care that the existence of evil and the existence of God are incompatible? Don't you know that God can do anything? He can make contradictions true. So your proving that the existence of God implies a contradiction is not a problem for God. He just makes that contradiction true." In order even to try to argue that God does not exist, you have to assume that God cannot do contradictions. So the claim that God cannot do contradictions is not where the theist sneaks in a loophole.

The best way to think of these things is to hold that the fact that God is all-powerful does not imply that he can do impossibilities. So there are limits—logical limits—to what an all-powerful being can do. So premise 3 of the original argument is false. We will want to adjust it to make it true. In order to make that premise true, we should rewrite it as follows:

3* There are no *nonlogical* limits to what an all-powerful, all-knowing being can do.

Let's look at premise 4: A good being always prevents evil as far as it can. Is this one true? At first look it seems like it might be true. Certainly good beings are *against* evil, and any good being would want to get rid of evil. But does a good being *always* prevent evil as much as it can? The answer is no. Sometimes a good person allows evil even when he could prevent it. Does this make the person less good? Not necessarily. A good person can allow evil and still be good *if* he has good reason to allow it.

Think of a parent. Suppose I give my son an allowance (which I don't). Suppose I gave him a dollar a week (which I wouldn't). Now suppose he takes his dollar and buys bubblegum with it. After a day he has chewed the gum and gotten it stuck in his hair (which he would). Now he wants a ball. So he comes to me and says, "Please, pleeeeaaasseee! Buy me a ball!" I might not buy it for him even though I *know* my refusal will cause him pain. Does this make me a bad parent? *He* might think so, at least for the moment. It does not make me a bad parent. You see, I have a good reason not to buy the ball. Actually I have at least two good reasons. First, I want him to learn how to manage his money. Second, I want him to learn that he does not get what he wants by whining and begging. Do I allow or even cause some evil? Yes, I do. But allowing this evil does not count against my goodness because I have a good reason to allow this evil. So premise 4, as it stands, is not true. It is not true that a good being always prevents evil as far as it can. We can adjust it to make it true, however. The true version will be something like the following:

4* A good being always prevents evil as far as it can *unless it has a good reason to allow the evil.*

We have seen that two of the premises of the original argument— proposed by Mackie—turn out to be false. We can, as we discussed, adjust them to make them true. If we do so, can we derive a contradiction? Let us check. The adjusted argument goes like this:

1. God exists and is wholly good, all-powerful and all-knowing.

2. Evil exists.

3* There are no non-logical limits to what an all-powerful, all-knowing being can do.

4* A good being always prevents evil as far as it can unless it has a good reason to allow it.

From these premises we can continue:

5* *If (1) and (4*) are true, then* God prevents all of the evil he can prevent unless he has a good reason to allow it.

6* *If (1) and (3*) are true, then* God *can* prevent **all** of the evil that it is logically possible to prevent.

7* *If (5*) and (6*) are true, then* God prevents all evil that is logically possible to prevent and that he has no good reason to allow.

8* *If (7*) is true, then* there is no evil unless it is logically necessary or God has a good reason to allow it.

9* *If (2) and (8*) are true, then* there is evil and there is no evil unless it is logically necessary or God has a good reason to allow it.

Statement 9* is not a contradiction. So we have shown that the adjusted argument does not provide a proof that God and evil are incompatible.

Mackie's argument to disprove the existence of God fails. Some of the important premises are false. Furthermore, if we adjust them to make them true, they do not support his conclusion. We can conclude at this point that one of the best arguments against the existence of God does not work. It is possible that God has a good reason to allow the evil there is in the world. If there is sufficient reason for evil, then evil does not count against God's existence.

Although we have successfully countered the original argument, we have done so at a price. The price is that we have to believe that God has some reason to allow the evil he does. This raises two issues. First, what reason might God have to allow the kind of evil we see in the world? We ought to have some idea if we believe that God does have a reason for the evil he allows.

The second issue actually results in another kind of argument against the existence of God. Even if we can think of reasons God could have to allow some evil, it seems like there are evils in the world that have no good reason. If it really does seem that there is no good reason to allow these evils, can't we conclude that, at least, it *seems* that God does not exist? In the next chapter, we will look at some reasons God might have to allow evil. In chapter twenty-one, we will turn our attention to the more difficult situations where there seems to be no good reason to allow the evil we see.

19

REASONS GOD COULD HAVE TO ALLOW EVIL

In chapter eighteen, we saw that the argument given by John Mackie to prove that God does not exist was not successful. It *is* possible for evil to exist even if God is wholly good, all-powerful and all-knowing. Evil can exist because it is possible that God has a good reason to allow evil. A good person, even a wholly good person, is not bound always to eliminate evil as long as he has a good reason to allow it.

While this fact alone is enough to show that the argument fails, it will help our case if we point out some of the reasons God might have to allow evil. It is important to keep in mind that we do not have to claim that we *know* what God's reasons are to allow any particular evil. What we are claiming is that we know some things that *might* be part of God's reason to allow some evil situations.

It is no surprise that the first candidate for a reason that comes to mind would be free will. Ever since the problem of evil has been around, there has been a discussion of human freedom as a relevant answer. Free will is a complicated topic in philosophy. (This is not to be confused with *Free Willy,* which is a not-so-complicated movie about a whale that went into too many sequels.) In order to explain how human freedom might be related to God's allowing evil, I need to begin by explaining what I mean by human freedom. These are pretty controversial points and there are a lot of disagreements over them among philosophers. In this chapter I will simply *state* what I think about free will and its relation to the problem of evil. In the next chapter, I will *defend* my position. One reason for splitting these two jobs into different chapters is that the defense of my view of free will is actually something separate from the problem of evil. If all you are interested in is the problem of evil and if you think I argue for my ideas sufficiently in this chapter, you can skip the next one. Well, maybe you had better not *skip* it. You may, after all, be graded on its content even though it is not exactly on the main topic. Anyway, back to our question.

What is free will? A better question is, when is an act free? In order for you to be free in a particular act, it must be the case (or so I am saying) that whether you perform the act or not is up to you. In order for the act to be up to you, it must be the case (again, I am only asserting this, I am not arguing for it) that it is within your power to perform the act or not to perform the act. We might want to say, to be a bit more precise, that it must be in your power to *decide* to perform the act and to *decide* not to perform the act. You can freely decide even if your performance of an act is ultimately prevented. So, suppose you are standing on the brink of a decision. In fact, suppose you are literally standing, say, at Dunkin' Donuts. You have to decide between the honey-glazed and the jelly-filled. In order for the choice to be up to you, it must be possible for you to choose honey-glazed and it must be possible for you to choose jelly-filled (which I wouldn't because I do not *like* them, but suppose it is you who are the one standing there and you like both honey-glazed and jelly-filled). If you choose honey-glazed and do it freely, it cannot be that there was some fact that occurred *before* your choice that made it inevitable that you chose the way you did.

One way to look at this is to think of history as something like a giant videotape. Suppose we could rewind the tape of the history of the world and play it again. Suppose, further, that we let world history run up to your decision in the Dunkin' Donuts and you choose the honey-glazed doughnut. If we rewind world history an hour or two and then let it go again, when we get to your point of doughnut decision, it still must be in your power to choose honey-glazed or to choose jelly-filled. Remember, we are not thinking about a real videotape so that it *must* come out the same way each time you run it. What we are thinking about is rewinding *history* and letting *it* run again. If the choice is up to you, then each time we rerun history up to the point of your choice, it is true that at that point it is in your power to choose jelly-filled and it is also in your power to choose honey-glazed.

If your choice of doughnut is up to you, in this way, your doughnut choice is a free one—even if the doughnut itself is not free. If every time we rewind world history, you wind up choosing the honey-glazed, then we will begin to suspect that your choice was not really up to you. Rather, your choice is determined by some event that happens in world history before you choose.

The idea of freedom I am holding here is called *libertarian freedom*. Sometimes it is also called *incompatibilist freedom* because this kind of freedom is not compatible with determinism. I will discuss determinism in more detail in the next chapter. For now we can hold that it is the idea that, given the way the world was in the past and the laws of nature, every event must occur as it does. There is a concept of freedom that is compatible with determinism, but I am not going to explain that or argue that the libertarian view is better. I am saving that argument for the next chapter. Here I am simply going to assert that this is what freedom is all about.

Doughnut choices are nice and it is hard to go wrong at a Dunkin' Donuts. No matter what you choose, it will be a pretty good doughnut (unless it has raisins in it). For the problem of evil, we need freedom in more important areas. What we need is *significant moral freedom*. In other words, we need to be free about actions that have moral import and are not trivial. We do not need *every* action of ours to be free as long as enough of the important ones are.

So what does it mean to have significant moral freedom in the libertarian sense? First, *free moral agents are able to choose between (or decide for) moral alternatives (good and evil) without being determined to choose one or the other.* So my action is free if it is up to me that I do it. If my choice to act in a certain way is determined either by the laws of nature or by God—or by anything other than me—then the choice is not up to me. Therefore, it is not free.

Second, this means that if God creates free moral agents, they must be able, by definition, to choose evil as well as good. He cannot guarantee that we never choose evil without his violating our freedom. Whether we choose to do what is right or to do what is wrong must be up to us. It must be within our ability to do either. A free moral agent whose will is determined to choose good is a logical impossibility. He is a contradiction. God, as we saw in the last chapter, cannot make a logical impossibility.

So if God is going to create people, he has two alternatives. He can create free moral agents and allow the possibility that they will do things that are evil and the possibility that they will not do things that are evil; or he can create *determined nonmoral nonagents* and guarantee that they will not do anything evil. What he cannot do is create beings with significant moral freedom and also guarantee that they will not do evil. So, if God wants creatures with significant moral freedom, he must allow the possibility of evil.

Why should God create free moral agents and risk evil? This is a good question. Is freedom such a good thing? Sometimes people claim that they would like the world better if there were no freedom at all and, as a result, a lot less evil. Is freedom worth it? It is hard for us to judge this. I think we can begin to see how important human freedom is when we realize that most of the things that make life worthwhile to us require the freedom of the will. Think of the things that make *your life* worth living. I bet some of these things (probably most of them) involve your making real choices.

I will give just three examples. First, without freedom, we would have no moral responsibility. Unless my action is up to me, I cannot be held responsible for the act. This basic fact is known to all children. "It was an accident!" is perhaps the fourth phrase we learn as kids. We learn it right after we learn "Mom, she's touching me!" If you slip on the ice and knock me over, I will think you are a klutz, but I will not blame you. If, however, you push me down on the ice, I will have a different opinion about you. The difference between the things we hold each other responsible for and the things that we do not hold each other responsible for is that the former are up to us and the latter are not. I will hold you responsible for your action *pre-*

cisely because I think it was up to you that you did it. If we do not have significant freedom, we cannot be held responsible for our actions.

That freedom is important to meaningful human life can be shown by a second example. Many of the choices you make, even if they are not moral choices, constitute your living your life in a way that is valuable to you. I call these kinds of things *personal projects and accomplishments*. I remember dreaming about what it would be like to study philosophy in graduate school. (You may think such a dream would be a nightmare!) After five years of part-time study for my master's degree and five years full-time for my doctorate, I am still amazed at the privilege of studying philosophy. This is the life I have chosen and it has more value to me because it is my chosen path. Whatever I accomplish in my chosen path is more significant to me because I have chosen these goals and tasks. The meaningfulness of your life-course to you depends in part on the fact that you make choices along the way. Because those choices are up to you and you are a significantly self-determining person, those choices enhance the meaning of your life.

A third example can be found in our personal relationships. Think about this question: what if your mother were paying your boyfriend or girlfriend *a lot* of money to go out with you? You would be repulsed. (Well, you *might* be repulsed. You might think that you could live with it. It depends how desperate you are.) For the relationship to be *meaningful,* however, it must be freely chosen. Every day, I choose to love my family and my friends. Because I love them by choice and it is up to me, those relationships are all the more meaningful.

So, we can see that some of the most important aspects of being human depend on human freedom. What would life be like without moral responsibility, your chosen personal projects and your deepest relationships? Human freedom is a great good. It is central to what it means to be a human being. In fact, many religions tell us that the purpose for which we were created by God is to have a love-relationship with God. This kind of relationship, as we have seen, requires freedom. I think it is not possible actually to desire that we have no freedom. To experience a life without freedom is to experience less than a fully functioning human life. Nearly every person thinks his or her life is valuable. If this is the case, we do value—greatly value—human freedom.

In order to make us with significant moral freedom, God had to allow the possibility that we would choose evil. He could not give us this significant freedom and then guarantee that we never do what is wrong. It makes sense, then, that one reason God might have to allow evil is to ensure human freedom. Human freedom is a great good. I am glad we have been made in this way.

Now, human freedom is not a sufficient reason for God to allow *every* kind of evil in the world. For instance, evils we call *natural* evils, which include things like floods and earthquakes, are not the results of the misuse of free will. At least, they are not *directly* the result of a misuse of free will. What reason might God have to allow these kinds of evils?

Again, I do not think we can know all the reasons, but there are some possible reasons we can know. One possible reason is *the regularity of cause and effect*. In order for any of our actions to be meaningful, we must be able to affect the world. If we could not make any difference to the world and if we could not predict the effects of our actions, it would be impossible to act meaningfully. If every time I threw a rock at you it turned into a feather, I would throw rocks just to watch the transformation. If it were impossible to injure myself mountain climbing, I would not even try to stay on the mountain. Furthermore, it would make no sense to attempt to do so. Performing actions in a way that makes sense requires cause and effect regularities.

The regularity of cause and effect makes possible our meaningful actions. It also makes possible situations in which the environment causes severe damage to persons. The very reason fire is useful is the reason it can burn down houses. The chemical construction of water that makes it biologically vital also makes it possible for us to drown. The fact that nature operates with causal laws makes life possible. It also makes possible these natural evils. So the regularity of causal laws is a good thing. Perhaps the reason God allows some natural evils, then, is the need for causal laws. I know I have only pointed this out as a possibility and I have not defended it very thoroughly. I think, however, that you can get the idea that it is possible and even plausible that God could have reasons to allow the evil he does allow.

The answer to the square circle objection that Mackie put forward is that God could have a good reason to allow evil. If there are good reasons to allow evil, then there is no contradiction between the existence of a wholly good, all-powerful and all-knowing God and the existence of evil.

In this chapter we looked at some reasons that God might have to allow evil. We saw that significant moral freedom requires the possibility of choosing evil. Furthermore, it turns out that this kind of freedom is central to what it means to be a fully functioning human being. Many of the valuable things about human life require such freedom. To the extent that human life is a good thing, freedom is well worth it. We also pointed out that the regularity of cause and effect is necessary for any kind of stable world. This regularity can explain some of the natural evils in the world. Again, I do not pretend to read God's mind. I do not know what particular reasons he has to allow the particular evils in our lives. These general reasons make it plausible to suppose that he does have reasons to allow evil. These reasons are such that we can affirm still that God is wholly good as well as all-knowing and all-powerful.

One result of the philosophical points we have been thinking about in the last two chapters is that very few philosophers (even atheist philosophers) support this kind of argument anymore. Rarely do philosophers argue that the existence of evil is not compatible with the existence of God. Most grant that they are perfectly compatible. William Rowe, who is one of the leading atheists working on the problem of evil, wrote a paper called "The Problem of Evil and Some Varieties of Atheism." In it he admits that the project of attempting to show a contradiction between the existence of evil and the existence of God is not likely to succeed. He does not think, however, that this fact solves the problem of evil. Rowe develops a different kind of argument against the existence of God based on evil. This argument needs a different kind of answer. I will present Rowe's argument in chapter twenty-one, "The Unicorn Objection." Before we look at it, I want to talk about free will and determinism as I promised. In the next chapter, I will say what I need to say about these topics and then get back to issues about the problem of evil.

FREEDOM AND DETERMINISM

A CHAPTER YOU MIGHT WANT TO SKIP

Suppose I drop an open box of Cheerios on my kitchen floor, as I do from time to time. The Cheerios scatter and roll around randomly until they finally stop, where they lie for several days until they get crunched under our bare feet. Where each piece of Cheerio stops rolling is random. Well, it *seems* as though it is random. It is random in the sense that I cannot predict where each will go or that there is no special reason why they land in one place rather than another. Nor do I much care where they land. Actually I do not think it is *really* random. Exactly where a particular piece of Cheerio lands depends on the friction of the floor, at what angle I dropped the box, how high the box was, as well as the rate of gravitational acceleration and all of that. In fact, it is not random at all. I think we tend to believe that the position of each piece of Cheerio is *determined* by all of these things (as well as many other facts that I left out). Given the laws of gravity and all of the physical facts about the Cheerios and my kitchen floor, the Cheerios each land where they must land. When we say the Cheerios land *randomly,* we mean only that we do not much care about all of the little details that determine where they land.

Many people have thought that what happens with Cheerios can be seen as a model for the entire universe. (We can call it the *Cheerios model of the universe.* Maybe it will catch on.) Given all of the facts about the universe and all of the laws of physics, *every event* is determined to happen, just like every piece of Cheerio lands where it must. The idea that every event is determined is called, not surprisingly, *determinism*. A hundred years ago or so, most scientists held the Cheerios model of the universe although none of them called it by that name. It was the going assumption that every event in the universe was determined in this way. Few scientists today believe that *every* event is determined. As we say in chapter eight, quantum events are thought to be not determined. I think most scientists think that most events, at least most medium-sized events, are more or less determined. There are, it is thought, exceptions.

Let us assume for a while that the universe is determined. I mean not just that most events are determined, but that *every* event is. We are assuming, then, that the Cheerios model of the universe is true. Given, on one hand, the way the universe is at some time and, on the other, all of the relevant laws of physics, we can calculate every particular event that will happen. Of course, we cannot *really* calculate every event. It is all too complicated for our small brains and slow computers. In *principle,* however, we can. So let us pretend that the universe is determined in this way.

Thinking about the universe as determined can help us think about the freedom of the will. If every event in the universe were determined in the way I just described, would any of our actions be free? Well, it all depends on what is required for an action to count as free. I want to argue that, if the universe is determined, *no* action of ours is free. I fear that this claim probably sounds too obvious even to mention. It is, in reality, quite controversial. In fact, throughout most of the history of philosophy and theology, it has been the minority position. Most thinkers believed that an act can be free even if it is determined.

Before you laugh out loud—or, maybe, while you laugh out loud—let me show why the majority position is quite plausible (even though I think it is wrong). The explanation goes like this. In order for one of my actions to be free, two things must be true of it. First, it must be the case that *I do the action in accordance with my will.* This condition means that I must do it because I want to. If I am forced—against my will—to do something, it is not a free action. So if you put a gun to my head and tell me to order vanilla ice cream rather than butter pecan, my ordering vanilla is not a free action.

The second condition for an act to be free on this view is that *if I did not want to perform the action, I would not have performed the action*. In other words, not only must it be according to my will, but it must also be the case that if my will were different, I would act differently. This second condition is important for cases such as the following. Suppose I am lying in my recliner in a blissful state of near-nap. The window is opened and a breeze is coming through. Somewhere in the distance, one of my more diligent neighbors is cutting the lawn, so the drone of the mower adds to the sweet springtime atmosphere. I say to myself, "Nothing suits me more at this time than to stay right here and not to move." Although I do not realize it, my daughter, Elizabeth, and her friend Ben from across the street have crept in while my eyes were shut and gently tied me to the chair. Clearly, I am staying in my chair according to my will. I want to be there. What is not true is that if I wanted to get up, I could get up. Because the situation fails to meet this condition, I am not staying in the chair freely. I could not move even if I wanted to, which I don't. An act must meet both of these conditions in order for it to be free.

The strange thing about these conditions is that an act can meet both of them and thereby count as a free act *even if the act is determined*. Suppose determinism is true. Suppose, further, that Elizabeth and Ben have not tied me up. I am sitting back in my recliner untied, but I am determined to sit there. Now just because I am determined to sit there with my feet up does not mean I am doing so against my will. I am determined to sit in accordance with my will. All of the motions of particles that form a vast causal network make it inevitable that I will sit in the chair. All of those motions determine me *through my will*. In other words, I am determined to have the desires I have. (Saying that the whole universe is determined includes the idea that everything in me is also determined—since I am part of the universe.) So, all of the motions in my brain cause me to want to sit back in my recliner. I am sitting there because I want to. These motions of chemicals and the like in my brain are, in turn, caused by other things that happen. This causal chain goes back and stretches to events that occurred outside my body and before I was born. So, given the way every particle in the universe was in the distant past (say, the year 1900) and the way the laws of physics and chemistry go, I was determined to sit in the recliner. Furthermore, I was determined to have the very desires I did have. It is still the case that I am sitting in my recliner because I want to. So this action passes the first condition.

What about the second condition? If I did not want to be sitting in the recliner, would I not be sitting? It might help us think about this second condition if we introduce a way of thinking about different possibilities. Sometimes, philosophers talk about different ways the world could be by using the term *possible worlds*. A possible world is a way the world could be. Suppose I had four children instead of three. If I had four children, other things would be different. I would be even more tired than I am now. Our grocery budget would be different, and there would probably be more broken down toys in our basement (if that is even possible). We are describing a possible world, the possible world in which I have four children. In the actual world, I have three children. The actual world is also a possible world. It is not, after all, an *im*possible world.

Understanding this use of the term *possible world* will help us figure out the second condition for an act to be free. Remember, if determinism is true, it is not only the position of my body that is determined, but every event is determined. Even my desires are determined. Remember also that I sit in the chair freely only if it is the case that if I did not want to sit there, I would not. For example, it must be true that if I wanted to get up and cut the lawn instead of sit in the chair, then I would get out of the chair. If determinism is true, can I have desires that are different than the ones I actually have? Sure I can. If the world were different in certain ways, I would have different desires. In some possible world, instead of having the desire to remain in the recliner, I have the desire to get up and cut the lawn. In the actual world, I want to stay in the chair. (I like the actual world better.) How does this work? If I am going to have a different set of desires and if determinism is true, I must be determined to have those desires.

"Wait!" you say (or you *should* say). "If you are determined to have the desire to stay in the chair, how can you be determined to have the desire to get out of the chair?" Remember what determines your desire is the way the world was a long time ago and all of the relevant laws of science. In the actual world, the way the world was a long time ago determines that I have the desire to stay in the chair. In some other possible world, the universe was different a long time ago. Maybe it was not very different, but it was different enough. Given the way the world was a long time ago in the other possible world and given the laws of science (let us pretend the laws of science are the same in all possible worlds, even though I think they are different in some possible worlds), I am determined to have a different set of desires. In that world, I am determined to have the desire to cut the lawn.

Maybe a picture will help. Suppose we make a diagram of two different possible worlds and their histories. We will picture the world's history as a line.

World 1.

1900	2004 (last Sunday)	
The state of the world in world 1	Desire to sit	Sitting

World 2.

1900	2004 (last Sunday)	
The state of the world in world 2	Desire to cut grass	Cutting grass

Figure 1

These pictures are of two different possible worlds. If determinism were true in each of the worlds we are considering, both my desires and my actions would be determined by the state of the world in 1900 and the laws of science. If the laws of science were the same in both worlds, then the only way I would have different desires and perform different actions is if the state of the world in 1900 (or any other date) were different in each world. Let us bring this discussion back to the conditions for a free action. Is it true that if I wanted to get out of the chair I would get out? Yes, it is. In those possible worlds in which I am determined to have the desire to get out of the chair, I would get out of the chair—assuming, that is, that nothing else interferes with my action.

So we have an action that is free even if it is determined. I sit in the chair because I want to and if I did not want to sit in the chair, I would not. If these two conditions are all we need for an act to be free, I can be free to sit in the chair even if I am determined to do so. What more could we want in order for an action to count as free? After all, I perform the act strictly according to my will, and if I didn't want to do it, I wouldn't. It sure sounds like a free act. This, then, is the majority position. An act can be both free and determined because it can meet the two conditions for freedom even if it is determined.

I do not think that the majority position is right. I think these two conditions are *not* enough for an act to count as free. I think there is something more that is needed. In order for me to be free in a particular act, it must be the case (or so I am saying) that whether I perform the act or not is *up to me*. Now, *up-to-me-ness* is not a very precise concept. We can get a bit of a handle on it by noting that if I am determined to sit in the chair, whether I do so or not is in no way up to me. It is true that I sit in accordance with my desires, but my desires are not up to me. I have the desires I have because of a lot of things completely outside my control. None of these things are up to me, and they determine what I want and what I do. If I am determined in this way, nothing I do is up to me. I have no control over any of my actions.

In order for my action to be free, I am saying, it must be the case that at the time of my decision, what I decide is up to me. It is in my power to decide to sit in the chair and it is in my power to decide to get up. Another picture may help:

Figure 2

A. 1900 and the state of the world at that time

B. the time I decide between sitting in the chair and getting up

C. the decision has been made and I sit in the chair

D. the decision has been made and I get up

Notice that in this diagram, the history of the possible world *branches*. We have a *C* world and a *D* world. Both the *C* and *D* worlds share the same history up to point *B*, when I decide to sit in the chair (or to get up). If I decide to sit in the chair, I *actualize* the *C* world. If I decide to get up, I actualize the *D* world. Which world becomes actual is, in this way, up to me. If determinism were true, we would not have branching worlds in this way. We might have parallel worlds, as in the first picture. (Parallel worlds, incidentally, have nothing to do with parallel universes as in science fiction.)

The power to actualize branching worlds sounds pretty dramatic until we realize that it means only that we have the power to choose between alternatives. If I choose one, I do not choose the other. The world, then, is different than it would have been. If I stay in my chair, the world is different than it would be if I had gotten up. What the world is like, in small ways such as this one, is up to me. The idea of freedom I am holding here is called *libertarian freedom.* Sometimes it is also called *incompatibilist freedom* because this kind of freedom is not compatible with determinism. None of my actions are up to me if they are determined. Hence, if any of my actions are free in this sense, not every event is determined. Therefore, determinism as a claim about the whole universe is false.

Now, why should you agree with me about the nature of human freedom? Let me give you two reasons. First, it seems strange to hold someone morally responsible for an action if that action is not up to him. If determinism is true, then no action is *up to* the one who does it. At least no action is up to the one who does it to a high enough degree to make it reasonable to hold the person responsible. Yet we do hold each other morally responsible. The best explanation is that some actions are up to us and we are responsible for them.

Second, libertarian free will makes the most sense of our deliberation. We often find ourselves deliberating between alternatives, and we are convinced that our deliberation has a real effect on the outcome. The decision we come to, upon deliberating, seems to be up to us. If freedom is not of the libertarian kind, then deliberation does not make as much sense. Thus, libertarian freedom is the better concept of freedom, and compatibilist freedom is no freedom at all.

21

THE UNICORN OBJECTION

Have you ever seen the movie *The Princess Bride?* There is a great scene in which the Spanish swordsman, Inigo Montoya, finally finds the six-fingered man who killed his father. Inigo chases him through the corridors of a castle. In the dining hall, the six-fingered man turns and throws a knife at him. Staggering from the wound, Inigo pulls out the knife as the six-fingered man approaches to thrust his sword for the final kill. Inigo, weak from bleeding, barely deflects each thrust. In fact, he does not deflect them all the way. Each of his arms is stabbed.

Leaning against the wall and bleeding, Inigo is in a defensive position. All he is trying to do is prevent the six-fingered man from killing him. Because of this, he needs only to knock the sword aside. It is important to note Inigo's position. As far as our discussion of the argument from evil is concerned, we are in a similar position, although there is less blood. We are making only defensive moves. Grasping this point is important because showing that John Mackie's argument *against* the existence of God has failed is not the same as giving an argument *for* the existence of God. It is, as Inigo Montoya would tell you, no small thing to make a successful defensive move. Just as Inigo had to deflect several thrusts of the sword, our disposing of Mackie's argument is not the only defensive move we need to make. There is another thrust coming.

Before we look at that thrust, let us reflect a bit on how successful our first defensive move actually is. I mentioned that most atheist philosophers today think the kind of defensive move we have made is entirely successful. As an example, I mentioned William Rowe, who has written a great deal on the problem of evil from an atheistic perspective. Now if Professor Rowe is correct, then we have successfully warded off the first thrust. If you were to read Rowe's article, you would find another thrust coming. Rowe agrees that the square circle objection does not work, but he puts forward another objection to belief in God in the face of evil. We could call this objection (although Rowe does not use this name) the *unicorn objection*. In fact, I just did call it that. What philosophers usually call it is the *evidential problem of evil*.

Remember that our answer to the square circle objection is based on the claim that God could have a good reason for allowing evil. If it is possible that God has a good reason for allowing evil, then the existence of God and evil together is not like a square circle, and the argument is defeated. The evidential problem of evil takes up a different question. The question is *whether it is likely* that God has a sufficient reason to allow the amount or the kinds of evil we see.

There are evil things that seem to be so bad or so random that it is hard to believe that God has a good reason to allow them. Even if we grant that the existence of evil in general does not contradict the existence of God, when we look at some particular evil events in the world, they seem to be too horrible to have a reason. We can give examples, such as the long and painful illness that many people suffer, or some atrocious crime that rips a family apart, or an earthquake that wipes out a whole city. To look at the earthquake case for a minute, you might admit that we can figure out reasons God may have to allow earthquakes to happen from time to time. It is another thing entirely to try to figure out his reasons for allowing this particular earthquake to be so strong and to kill so many people. Whatever reasons he has to allow this to happen, it seems as though God could accomplish everything he wants to accomplish even if the earthquake killed one person fewer. It does not look like God could have reasons for allowing the exact extent of such evils.

Now if we remember our answer to the square circle objection, we should see that we might be in some trouble here. We said that God can be good and still allow evil if he has a good reason to allow it.

(Let us call a good reason to allow evil in general or to allow some particular evil a *justifying reason*.) If there are particular evils such that there is no reason that God could have to allow them, then God does not exist. Since it *seems* like there are evils of this kind, then it *seems* (at least) that God does not exist. Again, we will turn this hunch into a more precise argument. I have rewritten this argument to make it a bit simpler than Rowe's original version.

1. If there is unjustified evil (evil for which there is no reason sufficient to justify God in allowing it), God does not exist.

2. Probably there is unjustified evil.

3. Therefore, probably God does not exist.

Just like Mackie's argument, this is a valid deductive argument. In other words, the conclusion follows from the premises. If the premises are true, the conclusion must be true. There are, however, two important differences between Rowe's argument and Mackie's. The first difference is that the conclusion in Rowe's argument is a probable conclusion. He does not claim to prove that God does not exist. Rather he is giving an argument that *probably* God does not exist. What does the word *probably* mean in an argument like this one? As we discussed in chapter ten, there are different kinds of probability. How do we know what kind of probability Rowe has in mind? Well, we can tell by looking at the second premise. He does not cite or calculate any statistics in his probability claim. Rowe has not made a mistake here; there are no such statistics available. So the kind of probability he has in mind is the *for-all-we-know* type of probability. (Philosophers call this type of probability *epistemic probability*.) Rowe is saying that when we look at some particular evils, given all we know, it seems more reasonable to believe that there is no justifying reason to allow them than that there is a justifying reason. The same kind of probability comes into the conclusion that is in the premise. Therefore, for all we know, there is no God. It might be that we have not figured it out right, but as far as we have figured it out, it seems like God does not exist. So even if we are wrong and it turns out that God does exist, Rowe has argued that it is more reasonable for us to believe that he does not.

The second difference has already been mentioned. Rowe's argument relies on our looking at some particular instance of evil and trying to figure out whether there is a justifying reason for *that* evil. Mackie's argument, remember, was about evil in general. Rowe's argument is about particular evil. We look at such an evil occurrence, and we look to see if we can think of any justifying reason for God to allow it. It is no surprise that Rowe picks a difficult case. He tells the story of a fawn that is trapped in a fire that was caused by lightning. It is burned horribly and lingers for several days before it finally dies. The suffering of the fawn is a case of evil for which, Rowe claims, it is probable that there is no justifying reason. It sure looks like there is no reason to allow the suffering to go on. Human freedom is not relevant. The cause-and-effect regularities would not be affected, Rowe claims, if God stepped in to end the fawn's suffering. It looks like there is no reason to allow the evil.

I have named this argument "the unicorn objection" because the atheist is saying that something probably cannot be found. That thing is a reason that God could have to allow that evil. Just like a unicorn, a justifying reason for the fawn's suffering, it is claimed, will always elude us. Rowe admits that there *could be* a justifying reason for this evil. We cannot figure it out, but there might be a reason all the same. Even if there is a justifying reason for the fawn's suffering on this occasion, Rowe points out that there are countless other evil events just as perplexing as this one. Surely, there is not some hidden reason in *each* of these cases, is there?

You can see how strong the hunch is behind this argument. Let us pay attention to the details of the argument as a way to analyze it. We already said that it is a valid argument. If the premises are true, then the conclusion follows. Now are the premises of this argument true? The first premise is one we might have to accept. If we do not accept it, then we have to go back and rethink our answer to Mackie's argument. For the time being, at least, we will assume the first premise is true. (*I* do not want to go back through that argument again.) The second premise is the more important one. Is it true that there is evil that is unjustified? Of course, a careful look at premise 2 reveals that it is not claiming that there *is* unjustified evil. The premise is a less ambitious claim. It claims that as far as we know, there is unjustified evil.

Before we turn to this premise (something we will do in the next chapter), I want to urge you to reflect on Rowe's argument. Do you think the premises are true? If they are true, then probably God does not exist. In other words, all we know about evil in the world makes it more likely that God does not exist than that he does. Evil, then, would be good evidence against the existence of God.

22

IS THERE AN ELEPHANT IN THE ROOM?

In the last chapter, we looked at an argument proposed by William Rowe. The argument tries to show that it is pretty likely that there are some cases of evil for which God could have no justifying reason. If there are cases of evil for which God could have no reason, then God does not exist. We called this argument (although Rowe did not) the unicorn objection. We called it by this name because the argument does not try to *prove* that there is no justifying reason for the evil in question. It tries to show that *most likely* there is no such reason. A good reason God could have, then, is like a unicorn. It is hard to find. It is so hard to find that, although it is not impossible that there is such a thing, it is not reasonable to believe that there is. It might help us evaluate this argument if we state it again:

1. If there is unjustified evil (evil for which there is no reason sufficient to justify God in allowing it), God does not exist.

2. Probably there is unjustified evil.

3. Therefore, probably God does not exist.

In the last chapter, we decided that we would accept the first premise. Although some philosophers have tried to argue against this premise, we do not want to do so. Our discussion will center, then, on the second premise. The claim is that, for all we know, there is unjustified evil. If this premise is true, then God does not exist.

It may be instructive to think hard about Rowe's fawn case (given in chapter twenty-one) to see if we can discern some reasons that may justify it. Although it is not an event caused by a free human action, there are other things that might apply. For example, it may be that the regularity of cause and effect cannot be tampered with to the degree necessary to eliminate these kinds of evils without rendering the world too chaotic. Another line of thinking that may be fruitful is to think about the biological function of pain in an animal such as a deer. Pain functions as a sort of alarm to spur the deer to immediate action. In Rowe's story, the deer is prevented from taking the kind of action needed to save its life. So, although the deer is unsuccessful, it may be that the general operation of the pain mechanisms is justified. I bring these ideas up simply to point out that even in Rowe's carefully constructed case, there may be reasons that we *can* figure out that may make us doubt that this case is a case of unjustified evil.

The strength of the unicorn objection hangs on this second premise. It is not clear that the premise is true. So, let us think about why anyone would think that it is true. There is really only one reason that supports it. We can make the reason clearer by putting it in the form of another argument. Remember, the claim is that *probably there is no reason sufficient that would justify God in allowing the evil in question*. The argument for this premise goes as follows:

4. It *seems* as though there is no reason sufficient that would justify God in allowing the evil in question.

5. Therefore, it is *probably true* that there is no reason sufficient that would justify God in allowing the evil in question.

Of course, if 5 is true, then the second premise of the original argument is true: Probably there is unjustified evil.

The reason that some people accept the premise is that it seems as though it is true. Why else would someone accept statement 5? We cannot prove that it is probably the case that there is unjustified evil. If we search for a justifying reason long enough, though, and we come up empty, we can begin to think that it is more likely that there is no justifying reason for the evil in question.

It is true that we might come to think that there is no justifying reason for some evil event after we have thought long and hard about it. The question we must address, however, is whether it is reasonable to conclude that there is probably no such reason. Given the premise that it seems as though there is no good reason to be found, can we rightly infer that it is probably the case that there is no good reason at all? Is this inference a good one? Furthermore, how do we tell when these kinds of inferences are good and when they are not so good?

Let us consider what kind of inference we are asked to make here. The general form (in which anything can be substituted for x) is the following:

6. It seems as though there is no x.

7. Therefore, probably there is no x.

Is this kind of inference a good one? Sometimes it is and sometimes it is not. Let us consider two examples. First, let us think about elephants. Take a good look around the room. Does it seem like there are any live elephants in the room? (I mention live elephants to rule out little statues of elephants or Beanie Babies and the like.) I bet that it does not seem as though there are any live elephants in the room. If this situation is the case, you can reason as follows.

8. It seems as though there are no live elephants in this room.

9. Therefore, probably there are no live elephants in this room.

This is a good inference. You are perfectly reasonable in looking around the room and saying, "It seems as though there are no live elephants here, so probably there aren't any."

Let us think about another example. Look around the room again. Are there any carbon 14 atoms in the room? You might shrug your shoulders and think, "It seems like there are no carbon 14 atoms in the room." Can you conclude that most likely there are no such atoms? It does not seem as though you can reasonably draw this conclusion. So the following inference is not so good:

10. It seems as though there are no carbon 14 atoms in the room.

11. Therefore, probably there are no carbon 14 atoms in the room.

Sometimes it is the case, you see, that inferences from "It seems like there is no x" to "Probably there is no x" are very good, and other times they are pretty bad. What is the difference? When is it a good inference and when is it bad? What is the difference between a live elephant and a carbon 14 atom? Well, there are lots of differences. The one that matters here is that elephants are large and carbon 14 atoms are small. An elephant is so large that if there is one in the room, you won't miss it. A carbon 14 atom is so small that no matter how long you look about you (provided you do not use the right kind of laboratory equipment), you will not discover it. I think I can make this difference clear in the argument.

When is the kind of inference we are talking about a good one? When can we reasonably go from statement 6 (It seems as though there is no x) to statement 7 (Therefore, probably there is no x)? We can make this move with a degree of confidence when the following sentence is true:

12. If there were any x's in the room we would probably know it.

Let's replace the x first with "live elephant" and then with "carbon 14 atom." We get the following:

13. If there were any live elephants in the room, we would probably know it.

When we replace x with "live elephant," we get a true sentence. If there were a live elephant in the room, we *would* probably know it. Now we shall turn to carbon 14 atoms:

14. If there were any carbon 14 atoms in the room, we would probably know it.

When we replace x with "carbon 14 atom," the sentence turns out to be false. I would have no way of knowing whether or not there is a carbon 14 atom in the room.

So arguing from

8. It seems as though there are no live elephants in the room.

to

9. Therefore, probably there are no live elephants in the room.

is a pretty good inference. Arguing from

10. It seems as though there are no carbon 14 atoms in the room.

to

11. Therefore, probably there are no carbon 14 atoms in the room.

is not a very good inference.

Let us leave the elephants and the atoms and go back to thinking about evil. More precisely, let us think about a *reason sufficient to justify God in allowing the evil in question.* Would such a reason, if one existed, be more like an elephant or more like a carbon 14 atom? Is it more reasonable to believe that I would be able to figure it out if it were there or that I would not be able to figure it out? Is the following sentence true?

15. If there was a reason sufficient to justify God in allowing the evil in question, we would probably know what it is.

I want to make an observation before I try to answer this question. For most of the evils we encounter, we *can* think of some reasons that would be sufficient to justify the evil. Remember our discussion of the freedom of the will and the regularities of a cause-and-effect universe from chapter nineteen in this section. While we admitted that there are some cases in which it seemed as though these two reasons were not applicable, they do apply to many cases of evil.

The point of bringing this issue up here is that our worries in this chapter apply only to a fairly small percentage of the evil things in the world. Probably, most of the evils we know about are such that we can see reasons that might be connected to them. So when we ask whether statement 15 is true or false, we are not asking about the majority of evils in the world. Our question applies only to some evils.

If we think about a case of this kind of mysterious evil, is it the case that *if* God had a reason to allow it, we would *probably* know what the reason was? I do not think so. At least I am pretty confident that there will be some number of evil things that we will not be able to figure out. Since God's knowledge and wisdom are so far beyond ours, it is eminently reasonable to suppose that he will have reasons for allowing evils in our lives that we cannot grasp. We can figure out plausible reasons for most cases of evil. There will still be some evil events the reason for which we cannot discern. This is exactly what we should expect if God exists. It cannot be counted as evidence against God. So even though it might seem, at first glance, that there are no good reasons to allow certain evils we see, this does not provide strong evidence that these evils are really unjustified.

I do not want to be accused of pulling some kind of trick here. If God exists, there will be many other kinds of things that he does, his reasons for which we have no idea. Many of these things have to do with our lives. I wonder, for instance, why he made us with bodies. I do not know the reason. I also wonder why he made the universe the way he did. There seems to be a lot of wasted space. He could have made it more like an English garden than like a Nevada desert. Both English gardens and Nevada deserts have their appeal. Both are beautiful in their own ways. What God's reasons are for choosing to make the universe the way he did is something I cannot figure out.

So I do not think that it is more reasonable to think that there is unjustified evil in the world. We are simply not in the position to make that claim. As a result, I think Rowe's argument is not and should not be persuasive. My conclusion is that another argument against the existence of God, Rowe's *unicorn objection,* is not very strong. There may be other arguments against the existence of God that start from observations about evil in the world. Our discussion may or may not solve those difficulties.

I also must note that many philosophers think that Rowe's argument is persuasive. They think that if God exists, we should be able to figure out how more of the evil we see in the world is justified. None of these philosophers, as far as I know, think that we should be able to figure out *all* of the evil we see. They think we ought to be able to figure out more than we can. There is enough mysterious evil to convince them that there must be at least some unjustified evil. For the reasons I gave, I do not think that their case is strong.

I have argued, in this section, that two of the more famous arguments against the existence of God based on evil do not succeed. The first argument—that the existence of evil is incompatible with the existence of God—is widely thought to be unsuccessful. The second argument is one about which there is more disagreement. If I am right, then evil can provide strong reason for thinking there is no God only if there is some other argument than the ones discussed in this section. (You may want to look at some of the books I recommend at the end of the book to investigate other kinds of arguments about God and evil.)

As far as our cumulative case is concerned, I have argued that there are good reasons to believe in God and that belief in God can survive the challenge of evil. My overall conclusion is that the reasons to believe in God outweigh the reasons not to. To be sure there are many more arguments for and against God's existence than the ones we have discussed, and there are many more details about the arguments we have discussed. We have gone, I think, as far as we can in a book of this size.

In the final section, we will turn our attention to thinking about what God might be like.

PART FOUR

BEGINNING TO THINK ABOUT WHAT GOD IS LIKE

In previous sections we have looked at reasons to think there is a person whom we call "God" and a particularly important reason to think there is no such person. I concluded (I do not presume to say what you concluded) that there are good reasons to think that God does exist. The reasons to think he does seem more persuasive than the reasons to think he does not. You might not agree with me. In case you do not agree, it might be helpful if I point out that you are not alone. Many other thinkers also hold that it is more reasonable to believe that God does not exist than to believe that he does. There are some, quite a few actually, who think that my assessment of the arguments is pretty much right. It is important that we allow ourselves the luxury to disagree about this assessment. We may disagree, though I would still try to persuade you and I hope that you would still try to persuade me. It is time, however, to move on from the question of whether or not God exists to the question of what God is like.

It may seem a bit odd, once I grant that you might not think that God exists, to lead you through a discussion of what God is like. I do not think it is odd. Here is why. Even if you do not think there is a God, it is worth it to consider what a being such as God must be like, if he did exist. Investigating this question, as the philosophers say, in a *hypothetical* way will shed light on a lot of the things we want to say *about* God. For example, by studying hard what God can do (if there is a God), we can learn some things about power and about action and maybe even about what is it for a person to cause something to happen. By thinking about how it is that God would know, given the traditional idea that God knows everything, we might learn a bit about knowledge and belief. We can use the concept of God, then, as a tool for understanding other things we want to understand. The concept of God has played a very important role, in this way, throughout the history of philosophy.

We can do our thinking about what God is like, then, in a number of ways. We can begin with traditional thoughts about God's nature. The traditional notion of God is that God is a person. He is not just a force. He is not a person with a body like you and I are. He has no body but he is a person nonetheless. This idea implies that to be a person is not necessarily the same as being a human being. Every human being is a person, but there may be persons who are not human beings. Angels and intelligent aliens, if any exist, would count as persons who are not human beings. God has thoughts and intentions and he performs actions. He also knows things. Furthermore, he does things that are good because he is good. It is thought not only that God has these and other qualities, but that he has them to the ultimate degree. He knows things to the ultimate degree. That is, he knows everything. He can do things to the ultimate degree. That is, he can do anything he wants to do. He is good to the ultimate degree. He is morally perfect.

A different method is to begin with the conclusions of the chapters in this book and see what God might be like if we add all of them up. Now I think we will wind up somewhere near the traditional view of God. For example, if the arguments about the cause of the existence of the universe are any good, then God is a person who acts and who has lots of power. If the arguments about moral reality are good, or if the challenge about evil is even worth considering, then God must have a moral nature.

These conclusions are the starting points for the task of what we might call *philosophical theology*. There are many aspects to philosophical theology, but the aspect we are pursuing here is that of thinking philosophically about what theology might tell us about God.

In the chapters that follow, we will begin with the traditional view and take up three main questions. Depending on how our discussion goes, of course, I may throw in a few more questions along the way. The questions we will begin with are the following: First, what can God do? Second, what can God know? And third, does God communicate?

Along the way we will look into the nature of knowledge, the nature of space and time, and the nature of logic and language. You can see by this list that the question of what God is like (if he exists) does raise some of the central questions in philosophy.

24

WHAT CAN GOD DO?

W hat can God do? The short answer is everything! God can do everything. If God cannot do everything, then the problem of evil might be less of a problem than many think. Perhaps some evil cannot be prevented by God because he is not powerful enough. The problem of evil as it has been put forward over the years begins with the assumption that God is all-powerful. The technical term for this quality is *omnipotence*. God, we say, is *omnipotent*. If God can do anything (and everything), there may not be much to say about this topic. This chapter may turn out to be a short one.

I suspect that *you* suspect that it will not be too short. (Perhaps you are thinking that it will not be short *enough*.) By now, you have realized that there is always more to say, and you have learned that I am not going to bring up a topic unless the topic has some interesting twists and turns. Well, your suspicion is right. There are some twists and turns in thinking about what God can do.

We have covered some of the twists and turns very briefly before, when we talked about the problem of evil and whether there are any limits to what an all-powerful being can do. It will not do us any harm to rehearse a little of that discussion before we try to amplify it. Remember, in chapter eighteen I said,

> What does it mean that God is all-powerful? Can he do anything? *Can God make a rock so big that he can't move it?* (What about this one—*can God make a class so boring that even he*

falls asleep?) Some people think this question is one of the basically unanswerable questions. I can answer it. In fact the answer is pretty easy. Here it is. *No, he cannot!*

There. That was not too difficult, was it? Wait a minute! If God cannot make this rock, then he is not all-powerful, right? Again, the answer is no. Let me explain. A physical object that is so big that an all-powerful being cannot move it is a contradiction. There cannot be such a thing. It is like a square circle. So God cannot make one. You see, to say that God is all-powerful does not mean that God can do any task I can name in words. It means that he can do anything that is not a logical contradiction. A square circle is a logical contradiction. It is a logical impossibility. It is not a genuine possibility. It is really not a thing at all and therefore it is not surprising that God cannot make one. It is not a real limit to God's power that he cannot perform contradictions.

The best way to think of these things, we concluded, is to hold that the fact that God is all-powerful does not imply that he can do impossibilities. So there are limits—logical limits—to what an omnipotent being can do.

I pointed out, in the chapter on the problem of evil, some reasons we want to hold this position. I discussed these reasons in the context of the particular argument about evil. What we want to do here is get a more general take on what is going on. What is it about logic that makes it the case that God cannot break its laws? What is logic anyway?

I want to get at this question in a backward sort of way. Imagine you are driving down the Merritt Parkway in Connecticut at about seventy-eight miles per hour. If your mother is in the car with you, she might say something like, "You cannot drive that fast here." It will not do for you to respond by saying, "Sure I can. I am doing it, aren't I?" You *can* drive seventy-eight on the Merritt, but you *may* not. There is a law that says you may not drive seventy-eight, but it is a special kind of law. This kind of law does not regulate your actual behavior. It regulates what is acceptable behavior.

Think of something you *can* do and something you *can't*. For example, I can eat a bowl of ice cream, but I cannot jump six feet high. I am thinking about the high jump in track and field. Most people can eat a bowl of ice cream, although some cannot. Few people can jump six feet high. What is the difference between those who can jump six feet high and those who cannot? For one thing, those who cannot jump six feet high probably eat more ice cream than those who can. For another thing, those who can jump six feet high have probably trained quite a bit to be able to do so. Although I cannot jump six feet, I *might* claim that I *could* jump six feet if I trained sufficiently. At my age, it might not matter how much I trained. I might never be able to do it, but it may turn out that I could.

Let's think of something else I cannot do. I cannot jump thirty feet high. I am not the only person without this ability. I think that no one can jump thirty feet high. Remember, we are talking about the high jump on Earth, at sea level. We are not considering how high people could jump on the moon where the force of gravity is one-sixth of the force of gravity here. So I propose that no one can jump thirty feet high. Just to be sure of our example, though, let us think about jumping a hundred feet. No one can perform this feat.

Let's think of one more thing that I cannot do. Let's consider some mathematical task. I cannot, for example, successfully balance the checkbook. I cannot do this, but it turns out that my wife, Jeanie, can. This task, then, is not, strictly speaking, impossible. Let us think of another mathematical task: the task of finding a positive whole number that is a square root of two. This task is more difficult even than balancing the checkbook. There is a square root of two, but it is not a whole number. Actually there are two square roots of two, but we will limit our discussion to the positive square root of two. The positive square root of two falls between one and two. So the task of finding the *whole* square root of two is not something that I can do. It is not because I am a mediocre mathematician that I cannot solve this problem. There is no solution to it. It is impossible to calculate the square root of two correctly and come up with a whole number.

OK, let's try one more. I cannot draw a square circle. To be more precise, I cannot draw a two dimensional flat-planed closed figure that has exactly four ninety-degree corners and four straight sides of equal length and also has exactly zero corners and zero straight sides. A square circle, you see, is a square. As such, it has exactly four ninety-degree corners and four straight sides of equal length. It is also a circle. It has, therefore, exactly zero corners and zero straight sides. A square circle has four corners and it has zero corners.

All of the tasks I have been considering are impossible for me to do except, of course, the ones involving driving fast on the Merritt and eating ice cream—two things that I do, it turns out, too often. I suppose I *could* successfully balance the checkbook under the right conditions. I cannot jump six feet high. I cannot jump thirty or a hundred feet high. I cannot calculate the square root of two (correctly) and come up with a whole number, and I cannot draw a square circle. We can lump the jumping cases together and we can lump the mathematical and geometric cases together. Even though these are all cases of impossible things, they are impossible for different reasons.

What is it that makes the jumping cases impossible? It is the way the world works. We call the way the world works the *laws of nature* or the *laws of physics*. Given the laws of physics and my athletic ability (which is affected by the amount of ice cream I eat), I cannot jump six feet high. No matter what my ability were, given the laws of physics, I would not be able to jump a hundred feet. Jumping a hundred feet high is *physically* impossible.

Calculating the whole square root of two is impossible also. That I cannot do it, however, has nothing to do with the way the world—the physical world—works. The laws of gravity or other laws of nature are irrelevant. It is not because the square root of two is too *heavy* that it cannot be a whole number. This task is impossible because of the laws of arithmetic. You might say that it is *mathematically* impossible.

Drawing a square circle is *logically* impossible. Note that it is not artistically impossible only. It is not because of some law of art—such as the law of perspective—that I cannot draw such a figure. It is not because of the laws of nature or even the laws of mathematics. The laws of logic are what make square circles impossible. Logic itself dictates that there cannot be a two-dimensional flat-planed closed figure that both has four corners and has exactly zero corners.

Logical laws and physical laws each share something that city and state laws do not. When a logical or physical law tells you that you cannot do something, then you cannot do it. When a city or state law (or even a moral law) tells you that you cannot do something, you *can* do it but you *ought not* do it. If we think about jumping a hundred feet high or drawing the square circle, we will not say, "Sure the law *says* I may not draw a square circle, but what if I do not want to obey the law?" Laws of the state or moral laws (and even laws or rules of proper manners) are the kinds of laws that we can break even if we should not. Laws of nature (including laws of physics, chemistry and biology) and laws of logic are the kinds of laws that we cannot break even if we tried.

I say that the problem about the square circle is a logical problem and not a mathematical one because it is a particular example of a general kind of problem. Things cannot have incompatible properties. Or, as Aristotle said, "A thing cannot both be and not be in the same way and at the same time." (Actually he said it in Greek, but I am told that it translates into this easier-to-read English version.) So a figure cannot both have four corners and not have four corners at the same time and in the same way. Aristotle added the "at the same time" clause to allow for change. Sometimes things start one way and end another. For example, my ice-cream bowl starts out by being full, but at a later time (not much later, mind you) it is empty. In a sense, then, it can be both full and empty. It cannot be both full and empty *at the same time,* however. He added the "in the same way" clause to get out of confusions over metaphors and using words with different shades of meaning. For example, Charles Dickens did not challenge Aristotle when he penned, "It was the best of times, it was the worst of times." Dickens might defend himself against the charge of contradiction by insisting, "In *some ways* it was the best of times, but in *other ways* it was the worst."

Aristotle's sentence has been called the *law of noncontradiction,* and it has been considered the starting point for logic. It is a basic law of logic. Laws of logic raise lots of questions. I want to discuss one that is foundational. Why should we think that the logical laws are really laws? Or, to put it another way, why think the truths of logic are true?

Laws of logic and mathematics are very basic. (Note that I am lumping laws of mathematics and laws of logic together. They may be different, but the difference will not be very important for our discussion.) Laws of physics are less basic. Laws of the state are even less so. We can imagine a state with different laws. Physical laws are the same in every state. In fact they are the same all over the universe. Even so, we can imagine a universe that had no gravity or one in which the force of gravity was much weaker than it actually is. Logical and mathematical laws are even more basic. They are the same across universes—even imaginary ones. We cannot imagine a universe with different laws of arithmetic. Imagine a universe in which there were no physical laws at all. For example, if there never were a physical universe, there would be no physical laws. We cannot imagine that there were no mathematical or logical laws. Even if there were no physical laws, it would still be the case that $1 + 1 = 2$ and that contradictions cannot be true. Nothing about the *existence* of the universe or its *physical characteristics* make it the case that $1 + 1 = 2$ is true and that every contradiction is false. In contrast, it is precisely because the universe exists and has the physical characteristics it has that gravity operates the way it does. For example (here's a quick physics lesson), the force of gravity between two objects diminishes as the distance between the two objects grows. The relation between the force and distance has been discovered. The force of gravity between two objects is proportional to $1/d^2$, or one over the distance between the objects squared. If the distance between two objects is doubled, the force of gravity between them is reduced to a fourth of what it was previously. If the distance is quadrupled, the force is reduced to a sixteenth. This relation is called the *inverse square law*. The universe could have been different, however. It could have been that the force of gravity was proportional to $1/d^3$ rather than $1/d^2$.

Even if gravity operated by the inverse cubed law ($1/d^3$), it would still be the case that contradictions could not be true. So you can see that physical laws are less basic than logical and mathematical laws. No matter what the physical laws are, the logical laws will remain the same.

Another way to see the relationship between the different kinds of laws is to think about them, in a way, *geographically*. The speed-limit laws are quite local. They change from state to state and even from place to place on the Merritt. (I am afraid that at no place on the Merritt is it permissible to drive seventy-eight miles per hour.) Laws of physics are global. They work the same way all over the world. In fact, they are universal. The whole universe operates with the same laws of physics. Speed-limit laws also change with time. It used to be that the speed limit on stretches of I-95 was seventy. In 1973 (the year of the first gas crisis), all of the high speed limits in the country were lowered to fifty miles per hour. After a brief time, they were raised to fifty-five. Much later, they were raised in some places (not the Merritt) to sixty-five. Physical laws do not change with time. They are the same throughout the history of the universe. I have been told that some physicists think the laws of physics did not hold during the first few moments after the big bang. After that brief time, however, these physicists hold that they have been stable.

Laws of logic and of mathematics are even more stable than physical laws. They are not only universal but *necessary*. Not only do they hold throughout this universe (in all of its space and its time), but they hold in any possible universe. No matter which way the universe turns out (even if there is no space-time universe at all), the laws of logic hold. So, you can see why philosophers think that they are the most basic laws.

How do these issues make a difference to the question of what God can do? Well, if God made the universe and set it up the way he wanted it, then he has control over the way it works. In other words, he has control over what physical laws are in place. He can, it would seem, interfere with those laws. They do not act as an obstacle to him because he set them up. This fact accounts for the belief that God can do miracles. He can interfere and make things happen that would be impossible if he left things to go the way the laws of nature indicate they will go.

Can God interfere with the laws of logic? Can he make a contradiction true? Can he make it the case that he knows everything, for example, and that he also does not know everything (in the same way and at the same time)? If he cannot make a contradiction true, then he is in some way subject to the laws of logic. If he *can* make a contradiction true, then . . .

Well, *I do not know what to say.* I was going to say that he is not subject to the laws of logic. The problem with drawing this conclusion is that *if God can make a contradiction true, there is no longer a reason to draw this conclusion rather than any other conclusion!* Allow me to explain.

When we draw a conclusion, we say something like the following: "Given what we said before, the following must be true." In other words, "Given what we said before, it is not possible that the following is false." I will use an example of a valid argument that we looked at way back in chapter seven.

1. All mammals are warm-blooded.

2. My children are mammals.

3. Therefore, my children are warm-blooded.

When we draw the conclusion, we are saying, "Given that it is true that all mammals are warm-blooded and that my children are mammals, it follows that my children are warm-blooded (or it is impossible that my children are not warm-blooded)." Another way to put it is, "Given the claim that it is true that all mammals are warm-blooded, the claim that my children are cold-blooded mammals is impossible." If God can make a contradiction true, then contradictions can be true. If contradictions can be true, then we can't conclude that "it is impossible that my children are not warm-blooded." Or, to put it another way, we can conclude that my children *are* warm-blooded but that it also *may be the case* that they are not. If a contradiction is true, then *nothing* is impossible. The things that are least able to be possible are contradictions. So if one of them is true, all of the other things we would normally think to be impossible are surely possible. If a contradiction is true and nothing is impossible, then logic is suspended. If nothing is impossible, then our whole practice of drawing conclusions is undermined. In the end, there can be no more rationality, and all assertions become meaningless.

How do all assertions become meaningless? Let us take a simple assertion such as, "My hat is in the car." Pretend that this sentence is true. If this sentence is true, then the following sentence has to be false: "My hat is not in the car." If the first sentence does not imply that it is *not* true that my hat is *not* in the car, then it cannot mean anything. If contradictions can be true, then the sentence "My hat is in the car" is perfectly compatible with the sentence "My hat is not in the car." Any sentence you want to assert is perfectly compatible with its opposite. Any sentence, then, becomes compatible with any other sentence. You see, then, every sentence becomes meaningless.

The truth of Aristotle's law of non-contradiction, then, does not rest on our abilities. It is not because of human weakness or limitations that no contradiction can be true. It is not because the universe has certain features or even that God made it a particular way. It is because of the nature of truth and reason itself. The nature of truth and the nature of reason are among the most basic things in the universe. Even God cannot tamper with them.

To say that even God cannot tamper with the laws of logic sounds like I am putting an external limitation on God. It sounds like I am saying that there is actually something more powerful than God himself. I do not think that the laws of logic are *external* limits on God. I think that the laws of logic are expressions of who God is and how he thinks. To say that the law of non-contradiction is most basic is another way of stating the simple fact that God is exactly who he is and he is not otherwise. I think that the most ultimately basic fact is that God is who he is and he is not who he is not. On this fact, I think, rests the law of non-contradiction. Logic, then, is not external to God and it does not have authority over him. It is a reflection of who he is.

Well, let's get back to our original question. What, then, can God do? God can do everything that is possible. He can make any kind of possible universe. He cannot make a logically impossible universe because there cannot be such a thing. It is no limit to his power but it is an expression of his character.

So if you are struggling to draw that square circle, take heart. Not even God can do better.

WHAT CAN GOD KNOW?

What can God know? The short answer is everything! God knows everything. If God cannot know everything, then the problem of evil might be less of a problem than many think. Perhaps some evil cannot be prevented by God because he does not know about it or because he does not know how to prevent it. The problem of evil as it has been put forward over the years begins with the assumption that God is all-knowing. The technical term for this quality is *omniscience*. God, we say, is *omniscient*. If God knows everything, there may not be much to say about this topic. This chapter may turn out to be a short one.

We have been through this before. In fact I nearly copied the first paragraph for this chapter from the first paragraph of the last chapter. And, like the last chapter, there will be twists and turns here, so let us cruise down the road and watch out for the turns! Here comes one now.

I propose that there is a sense in which we want to say that God cannot know *everything*. There are boundaries to his knowledge. Now, before you think that I am going to reject the traditional view, I want to assure you that I hold firmly that God is omniscient. How can it be that God is omniscient yet he does not know *everything*? In order to make sense out of these claims, we have to think a little bit about knowledge in general.

What is knowledge? What is it to know something? I will take it as obvious that we do know things. I am not worried about skepticism. For example, I think we know that George Washington was the first U.S. president. I think we know that the moon is far away and that it is not made of green cheese. We know that there are trees and birds and that the whole world did not pop into existence only five minutes ago with all of our apparent memories programmed into us. We know lots of things. What is our knowledge of these things?

Many philosophers today think that there are three basic ingredients to knowledge. That is, there are three ingredients to *human* knowledge. Whether God's knowledge will have the same ingredients remains to be seen. The first ingredient is belief. Knowledge is a kind of belief or, more accurately, it is a kind of belief that stands in certain relations with other things. Now, not every belief counts as knowledge. Sometimes our beliefs are false. A false belief cannot be knowledge. You would not want to say, "I know *x*, but it is false that *x*." We cannot know false things. In order to count as knowledge, then, the belief must be true. Truth is the second ingredient to knowledge. So I cannot know that Thomas Jefferson was the first U.S. president. No one can know this because it is not true that Jefferson was the first president. So far, then, we have the idea that knowledge involves a belief that is true.

Sometimes we *contrast* belief with knowledge. If you ask me where your keys are, I may say that I believe they are on the table. If you ask, "Do you know they are on the table?" I may say, "I do not *know* they are on the table, but I *believe* they are." Belief seems to be opposed to knowledge. In cases such as this one, I think what we are opposing is not knowledge and belief but knowledge and *mere* belief. Even if it is true that your keys are on the table, we will want to contrast mere belief with knowledge. It must be, then, that only some true beliefs can count as knowledge.

This position seems right. Lots of my beliefs turn out to be false. The keys might have been in your pocket all along. Other beliefs might be true, but we still will not want to say that they are cases of knowledge. Suppose you flip a coin and I believe that it will come out heads. That is, I really believe that it will and I am not just saying that I believe that it will. Suppose it does come out heads. Did I *know* that it would? I don't think so. It was a belief and it was shown to be a true belief, but it was a lucky guess.

In order to grasp what knowledge is, then, we have to have some way of keeping lucky guesses out of the cases of knowledge. Philosophers have often used terms such as *justification* to pick out this third thing that goes into constituting knowledge. On some accounts, a case of a person's knowing something is a case of her believing it, its being true and her being justified sufficiently in believing it to be true. Justification, then, is the third ingredient to knowledge.

Justification is the ingredient of knowledge that has most given philosophers their sleepless nights. For the past forty years or more there has been a major preoccupation with figuring out what it takes for a person's belief to be justified. There are lots of differing theories about this idea. Some people think that my belief cannot be justified unless I have the right kind of evidence for its being true and unless I know what this evidence is. These philosophers often argue about what makes for good evidence. Other philosophers think that I can be justified even if I am not aware of any evidence for my belief. I am justified if my belief is formed or sustained in the right way. Still others argue that justification is a problematic concept and that there is something else at work in cases of knowledge. These arguments are pretty important in philosophy in general. They are much less important for thinking about what God knows because God is not limited the way we are limited. He probably has all of the justification he needs for anything he believes.

The sticky parts to thinking about God's knowledge have to do with the truth question (although I also wonder if God's knowledge consists of beliefs the way ours does). Are there true things that God cannot know? No one thinks that God can know false things. He cannot know 1 + 1 = 3 because it does not equal three. He cannot know how to draw a square circle because there is no way to draw such a diagram to be known. So when I said earlier that there are things that God cannot know, I was thinking of false statements. False statements cannot be known because in order to be known at all, a statement or claim has to be true. Of course God knows that each false statement *is* false, but this case is not the same as knowing the false statement.

The hard question, then, is, are there *true* things that God cannot know? If we say that there are true things that God cannot know, either we have to revise our understanding of omniscience or we have to say that God is not, after all, omniscient. He does not know everything that can be known. Some philosophers have made each of these moves. Others have insisted that he does know everything that can be known.

One potential problem involves statements you might make such as the following: "I am here now reading this book." Suppose this statement is true. In fact, I would bet that it *is* true. If you are reading, then you *are* reading. Furthermore, you are doing it exactly *when* you are and *at the same place* at which you are located. So when you say the sentence, "I am here now reading this book," you are saying something true. Can God know this? Certainly he knows that you are reading the book. (I am sure as well that he approves.) He also knows what time you read it and where you are when you read it. He knows you are lying on the couch in the living room, about to doze and drool. So perhaps God can know this true statement.

Let us look more carefully, however. The statement that you said (or the one *I* said that you said) is not exactly the same as the one that God knows. God knows, say, that you are lying on the couch in your living room at 4:00 p.m. on a particular Tuesday. Your statement did not say anything about the living room or what time it is when you are reading. What you said was, "I am here now reading this book." I want to look at two of the words in your statement and show how they each may cause problems for the idea that God knows everything that is true. There are certain similarities in the ways these two words function. The words are *here* and *now*.

Many words and phrases point to or pick out things. For example the phrases "author of this book" and "father of David, Nick and Elizabeth" both point to the same thing. That thing is me. (*Me* in the previous sentence also pointed to the same thing.) Names pick out the same things on most of their uses. So "George Washington" nearly always picks out the same person. There may be some other person named "George Washington." If there is, then sometimes the name

"George Washington" picks out that person. Usually, at least when I use it, it picks out the person who was the first U.S. president. Other words or phrases pick out different things with different uses. Consider the phrase "the current president of the United States." This phrase picked out the same thing every time I have used it since January 20, 2001, but after January 21, 2009 (and maybe before this date), it will pick out someone other than George W. Bush. Some words or phrases pick out different things on almost every use.

Shortly after I graduated from college, I drove with a bunch of friends from Maryland to Colorado. Up until that trip, I had never been further west than Ohio. Somewhere along I-70 in Kansas, driving west at about sixty miles per hour, my friend Glenn and I began to say, "This is the farthest west I have ever been. *This* is the farthest west I have ever been. No, *this* is the farthest west I have ever been." Each time we said, "This is the farthest west I have ever been," it was true. After awhile we annoyed everyone else in the car. Perhaps it is no surprise that some years later Glenn and I each did graduate work in philosophy.

Each time you use the word *this,* you point to something. It can be something different or it can be the same. Cruising down I-70 we pointed to the spot we had reached on the highway. Each time we said the sentence, we had reached a different spot. Of course we did not point with our fingers. We pointed with the word. The words *here* and *now* function a bit like the word *this.* Each time you use the word *now,* you point to a different time. So *now* in many of our sentences means something like "right when I say this sentence." *Here* means something like "right where I am when I say this sentence."

When we have a conversation and you say *here,* I might say *there* because I am not at the place you are. Of course, sometimes we use words like *here* and *now* to pick out big places and long times. So I might say, "Now we know that the sun is the center of the solar system." I do not mean just this second; I mean something like "in modern times" or "since Copernicus." If you are visiting from Japan and I say, "Here we eat lots of French fries," I mean the whole country, not just at my kitchen table.

OK. Let's get back to God. Why might it be a problem to figure out how God can know these kinds of sentences? Well, he is not in space at all. So no place is *here* for him. Perhaps it is better to say that every place is here for God because he has perfect access to each point in space. No point in space is further from his ability to act than any other point. When we say that God is everywhere, we have this sort of thing in mind. It is not that he is spread out in space like a fog but that every point in space is present to his mind and will.

If no place is literally here for God, he can still know you are reading here. We pick out what counts as *here* by reference to other things that are located around us. We do not think that there is some place that is *here* independent of who is thinking about it. *Here* and *there* are relative terms. The word *here* picks out different places depending on where the person who uses it is located. That God knows what you mean by *here* when you say it is enough. He knows that you mean on the couch in the living room. Now God cannot *be* at the same place that you say the sentence, but he knows your relation to the place that you point to with your use of the word *here*.

God's relation to space does not raise as much of a problem as his relation to time does. The traditional view is that God is not in time at all. He is outside time. Sometimes this view is called the *eternal view* or the *atemporal view*. I will call it *atemporal* because sometimes *eternal* gets used in various ways. What does it mean to think that God is atemporal? This claim has two parts. First, God exists but does not exist *at* any time. His existence is not located in time the way your existence is and my existence is. Second, God does not experience any succession. He does not experience one event before he experiences another. He does not experience George Washington's presidency before he experiences George W. Bush's presidency. To be sure, he knows that the one occurs before the other in time, but he experiences them both in one act of knowing.

The more widely held view, among philosophers at least, is that God is everlasting but in time. That is, he never came into existence and he will never go out of existence, but he is in time. He exists at each moment in time and he experiences things that happen in time sequentially. He does, on this view, experience Washington's presidency before he experiences Bush's.

If the traditional view is correct, then he cannot *be* at your *now*. He knows everything that happens at the time you say your sentence, but he does not experience it *as now* in the way you do. He experiences *every* point in time "all at once," so to speak. If God were to use the word *now* literally, he could not point precisely to one point in time as opposed to another point. For him, all times are now, just as each point in space is "here" for him. So he cannot really use the same sentence you use to express what he knows. He has to use a different sentence: "Fred" (pretend you are Fred) "is reading on the couch in his living room at 4:00 p.m. on Tuesday."

Does the fact that God has to use a different sentence imply that he does not know the same thing you know? This question is more difficult that it looks. Let me see if I can make its difficulty a bit clearer. I'll start with another look at space. If we list all of the things God knows about *where* you are reading this book, the list will be quite long. He will know a zillion statements of the following form: "You are reading at the same place as ____" and "You are reading exactly ____ inches from ____" (though I suppose God would use the metric system). He can fill in the blanks with any number of things that are near enough to you to count as being at the same place. For example, you are reading on the couch in the living room in your house in Hamden, Connecticut. You are reading exactly seventeen inches from the table with the lamp on it.

Now, if you know all of the facts on this list, do you know all of the facts about where you are reading? It seems as though you do. There is no additional fact that is missing such as the fact that all these things are *here*. The moral of the story is that God can know all of the facts about where you are even if he is not located in space. Can we make the same move as far as time is concerned?

If we list all of the things God knows about *when* you are reading this book, the list also will be quite long. He will know a zillion statements of the following form: "You are reading at the same time as ____" and "You are reading exactly ____ minutes after (or before)

_____ happens." He can fill in the blank with any number of events that are simultaneous with your reading (or before or after it). For example, you are reading at the same time that my son Nick is playing chess and at the same time that my son David is thinking of a new plot twist for the movie he is writing or twenty-one minutes before my daughter Elizabeth starts riding her bike. You are reading at the same time that some largemouth bass is eating a minnow rather than my fishing lure.

Now, suppose you know all of the facts on that list. Do you then know *all* of the facts about when you are reading? Time, to many philosophers, is different than space in this regard. They think that there is a *now* in addition to all of the facts about what else happens at the time in question. If this claim is true, you can know all the facts on the list but not know every fact about when you are reading. Philosophers have taken three basic positions about this issue.

The first two positions are ones that include the idea that there is a *now* in addition to all of the facts about what events happen when. Many philosophers who think so hold that the nature of time means that God himself must be *in* time. Only a temporal person, they reason, can know what is happening now. If God is not in time, then all times are now to God. If all times are now to God, then his relation to each point in time is the same as his relation to any other point in time. He does not have some special relation to the particular point in time that is now. He cannot pick it out. So if God is to know what is happening now, he must be *inside* time in some way. God himself must experience a now if he is to know what is happening now. Other philosophers think that time works this way but that God can know all facts about time even if he is not himself in time. These thinkers employ various strategies to reconcile God's knowledge of things in time with his being atemporal. Some of these strategies, I think, are fairly successful.

Other philosophers do not think time works in this way. They think there is no now apart from the events that occur. Time, for them, is more like space. They might reason as follows: when you say, "I am now reading this book here," you are picking out the time and place of your reading. You are picking them out in relation to where you are when you say the sentence. Tomorrow, when you are in the kitchen, you might say, "Yesterday, I read that book there." What makes each of these sentences true is the same fact. That fact is that at a particular time you were in a particular place reading the book. Both of these sentences express the same fact, but they get at that fact from different points in space and time. These philosophers will not have the same problem about God's knowledge. They also can hold that God can be outside time and still know that you are reading now.

As you can see, all three of these approaches to time allow philosophers to hold that God knows all true things. One result of holding that God knows all true things is that how we should think about God's relation to time is affected by what we think time itself turns out to be.

Either way, it can be held that God does know every truth.

26

CAN GOD KNOW THE FUTURE?

Did you notice what happened in the previous chapter? We began talking about what God can know and we wound up talking about his relation to time. I might as well admit that the same thing will happen in this chapter. These two issues have been tied up with each other throughout the history of philosophy. In this chapter we will worry over God's knowledge not of the present, but of the future. Which view about God's relation to time is better to hold? Well, the most important reasons for either position are related to his knowledge. As we saw in the last chapter, there are puzzles about God's knowledge of the present if God is not in time. It is hard to see how God can know facts about what is happening now that are independent of all of the facts about what other events are going on, if there are such facts, and still be outside time.

On the other hand, if God is in time in some way, it is hard to see how God can know what you will eat for breakfast tomorrow—that is, if you freely choose what you will eat. If God is in time, your breakfast-eating event is in the future to him, just as it is in the future to you. If God knows that you will choose to eat Cheerios, then it must be true, in some sense, that you will choose Cheerios. If *today* it is already true that *tomorrow* you will choose Cheerios, then it was true a hundred years ago that you will choose Cheerios tomorrow. If a hundred years ago it was already true that you will choose Cheerios tomorrow, then it can't be up to you what you have for breakfast. If you want to think about the kind of free choice I am talking about, you can review chapter twenty, "Freedom and Determinism: A Chapter You Might Want to Skip."

What you eat for breakfast seems to be a pretty clear case of something that is up to you, if anything is. If we decide that it is not up to you, then not much else will turn out to be up to you either. If God knows ahead of time what you will do, then what you will do is already in some sense *set*. It is not up to you.

There are three ways (at least) to try to get out of this fix. First, you can argue that God's knowing ahead of time what it is that you will do tomorrow poses no threat to those actions being up to you. Second, you can deny that God knows these things ahead of time. It is not that he fails to know what you will do. It is that he does not know these things in time. He does not know these things in time because he is not in time. He is atemporal. The third way to get out of this is to claim that God knows all true things but that there are not any truths about what you will freely choose in the future. So he does not know what you will have for breakfast tomorrow. Good philosophers have defended each of these positions.

Traditionally, the second strategy has been the most popular. Thinkers have argued that God is not in time and therefore he does not, strictly speaking, *foreknow* anything. He knows what you will eat for breakfast tomorrow but he knows this atemporally. The way that this is supposed to work is that, in God's consciousness, there is no past, present or future. He has knowledge of every point in time "all at once." It is more literally true to say that he knows every point in time in the same eternal moment (although the word *moment* might not fit literally here). God's knowledge of your eating Cheerios tomorrow is at once simultaneous with your eating them (tomorrow) and simultaneous with our speculating today about your eating them. (Of course, *simultaneous* also does not fit literally here.) That God knows your reading this chapter today in the same eternal moment in which he knows your eating Cheerios tomorrow does not make it the case that your breakfast choice is outside your control.

Let me unpack this view a bit more. What makes it seem as though your breakfast choice is not up to you is the idea that a hundred years ago, God already knew that you would choose Cheerios. So, tomorrow morning, you get up and stagger to the cabinet and stare at the breakfast cereal. There is a box of Cheerios and a box of Cap'n Crunch. Can you pick Cap'n Crunch? In order to do so, you have to change God's past beliefs. No human being can change the past. What happened a hundred years ago is not in our control. It looks like you are stuck with Cheerios.

If God is not in time, then you can choose Cap'n Crunch without affecting any of God's *past* beliefs. The problem of God's knowledge of the future, then, can be solved. Of course, we still have the challenges left over from the previous chapter about God's knowing what is happening now.

The question of God's relation to time is one that I will leave dangling. It is not that I don't have my opinions about it but that to go *any* deeper would require going a *whole lot* deeper. My purpose here is to show that sometimes each position that is an option has both advantages and disadvantages. Furthermore, smart people can disagree about how the advantages and disadvantages measure up. Therefore, smart people can persist in disagreeing about the issue.

When we cannot seem to reach agreement, the only thing to do is go get a bowl of Cheerios . . . or maybe Cap'n Crunch.

27

DOES GOD COMMUNICATE?

W e are nearly through this section and the whole book, for that matter. It is fitting to step back and comment on our procedure. I am going to make what will look at first like a fairly bold claim. I hope, once we think about it a bit, it will begin to seem more obvious than bold. Here is the claim: There are only two basic ways we can know anything at all about God. Wasn't that bold?

The first way we can know anything at all about God is by a method I call *inferring*. What I have in mind is that we first look around the universe and make lots of observations. This looking includes looking at ourselves. Then we infer what is most likely to be true about God as a result. The method of inference involves lots of little independent lines of evidence that add up to tell us if God exists (or if he does not) and what God is like. As we saw in chapter sixteen, this method is a little bit like the kind of reasoning a detective uses to pinpoint the identity of a criminal. Just as a detective will not normally rely on only one line of evidence, the method of inference allows us to use several different lines to lead to our conclusion.

Throughout this book we have relied on this first method in our attempt to think clearly about God. For example, we noticed that the universe is the kind of thing that did not always exist. There is good reason to think it began to exist. This implies that it may well have had a cause of its existence. (Remember we did not prove that it *had* to have a cause.) If it did have a cause, then that cause has lots of power compared to us. So we learn that it is likely that God is quite powerful. We also saw that there was good reason to think there are real moral values that are best explained by the existence and nature of God.

Now, I must point out that the method of inference may point in different directions. Many people think that observations about evil in the world point to the conclusion that it is more likely that God does not exist than that he does. So our thinking about the problem of evil in section three was a working out of this method of inference. The first way we can know anything at all about God is by inferring from what we observe around us.

The second way of knowing anything at all about God is if God steps into the world and *reveals* himself to us. Not surprisingly, I call this method *revelation*. It may be more accurate to call it *special revelation*. If God tells us true things about himself, then we have another way of knowing things about God. In the monotheistic traditions of Judaism, Christianity and Islam, it is claimed that this is precisely what has happened. Not only can we know things about God by observation and reasoning, we can know things because he has told us.

Notice that the first way to know anything about God moves from the world to God. The second way moves in the opposite direction. It moves from God to us. These are the only two directions to go and, I think, it might now be obvious that these are the only ways we could know anything about God. If our overall assessment of what we observe about the world and about human beings gives us good reason to believe he exists and has certain characteristics, then we gain good information about him. If God has revealed himself, we gain even more information about him. If God is real, we ought to expect that what we infer and what he reveals will fit together.

I am not going to try to argue that God has, in fact, revealed himself. I do want to think about the question and perhaps make the claim a little more plausible than it otherwise might have been. I realize also that the methods of inferring and revelation connect. Any particular claim that God has revealed himself will be something that is itself subject to investigation. We will not accept every such claim simply because it is made. We will want to search it out and find good reasons to think that the claim is reliable or good reasons to think that it is not.

Is it reasonable to think that God has revealed himself? If our application of the method of inferring in this book has been well pursued, our expectation can be pretty high that God *will* reveal himself to the human race. If God does exist and he created the world and he has the moral nature that we inferred, then he made us with a purpose. It makes sense that he would want us to know the nature of that purpose and how to pursue it. If we think that our purpose has to do with our relationship to the Creator, we are even more justified in expecting that he will reveal himself to us. Our expectations, I think, can be fairly strong that God, if he exists, will reveal himself.

How would God reveal himself to us? Suppose you are waiting at your house for your friend to show up so you can go with her to McDonald's. In the meantime, another friend comes by and suggests that you go instead to Starbucks. You decide to go to Starbucks, but you want your first friend to know where you are so she can meet you there. You have to figure out how to let her know where to meet you.

One way you can let her know is to count on her finding a trail of clues, including your footprints, outside your house leading in the direction of Starbucks rather than in the direction of McDonald's. Another way to let her know is to go to Starbucks and think deep and warm thoughts about your friend. You can hope that your thinking about her will make her get a feeling or a sense that you are at Starbucks rather than at McDonald's. Another thing you can try is to get a piece of paper and write a short note (saying something like, "Cindy, we went to Starbucks. Meet us there") and tape it to your door. Why does the third method work better than the first two? It does so because *language is the primary way we communicate content*. It is not the only way we communicate, but it is the primary way we communicate. We are language-using creatures.

Now, if God created us and has a purpose for us and wanted to communicate it to us, what method might he use? Many people seem to think that he will give us vague feelings about him and allow us to try to figure out what it is he wants to communicate from these feelings. I think he would probably use language. After all, he made us to be language users.

The main monotheistic religions in the world (Judaism, Christianity and Islam) have been called the "religions of the Book." Each claims that a particular text contains the written word of God. To contemporary ears, such a claim may seem very strange. I think it is not so strange. When we think about communication and human nature, it begins to make sense that God would use language in order to communicate. Putting that language into a book has several advantages. I will point out two. First, a book can preserve the record of God's revelation for other people and generations. God's revelation is not then left in the hands of the few who originally received it. Second, a book is a public sort of thing. It can be read, studied and analyzed by anyone with access to the book. Its meaning can be debated and different people can check their differing understandings against the text of the book. Thinking about human communication and the nature of books helps us see that the claim that God reveals himself through a book makes a good deal of sense, whether or not it turns out to be true.

There are only two basic ways we can know anything at all about God or about whether God exists. We infer what seems most likely to be the case from what we observe about the world and human nature, or God might reveal true things to us. In this book we have spent all our time inferring what seems most likely to be true about God. The further claim that God has revealed himself to us is quite important. I think what we have learned so far raises our expectation that he would reveal himself and makes it plausible to think that he would do so through a book. Evaluating whether God has in fact revealed himself and where that revelation is to be found, however, would take another book altogether. While we wait for that book to be written, I would encourage you to continue your search on your own.

SOME SUGGESTIONS FOR FURTHER READING

Well, you made it! You have made it through the entire text. That is, unless you flipped to the end and read this chapter first. I want to take stock of where we have been. In chapter one, I admitted that I have a secret dream. My dream is that I can help people learn how to think better. Now that we are at the end of the book, I ought to admit that I still have that dream. In fact, I hope that you have learned to think better as a result of reading and thinking about the chapters in this book. I hope that your experience in the practice of thinking will carry over to other important areas of your life, besides the questions about God. As a result of your exercise in thinking, you may find it more natural to ask some pointed questions of whatever it is that you are reading or watching on TV. If you do, I shall consider the book successful.

I also argued in the first chapter for the idea that thinking about God is something particularly important. I still think that this claim is true as well. I hope you have seen that you can make some progress by asking good questions and challenging obvious answers. Where do you go from here? I would encourage you to continue to think and to think hard about God as well as about every other important area of life. While I do not want to claim, with Socrates, that the un-examined life is not worth living, I think I can confidently assert that the examined life is the better life. It sure is a lot more fun.

If you are interested in digging a little more deeply into questions about God, I can recommend some very helpful books.

Murray, Michael J., ed. *Reason for the Hope Within*. Grand Rapids: Eerdmans, 1999.

Two chapters are especially helpful and cover in more detail some of the material in this book: chapter 3, "A Scientific Argument for the Existence of God: The Fine-Tuning Design Argument," by Robin Collins; and chapter 4, "God, Evil and Suffering," by Daniel Howard-Snyder.

Copan, Paul, and Paul K. Moser, eds. *The Rationality of Theism*. London: Routledge, 2003.

Chapters that amplify the material we have discussed include chapter 6, "The Cosmological Argument," by William Lane Craig; chapter 7, "The Teleological Argument," by Robin Collins; chapter 8, "The Moral Argument," by Paul Copan; and chapter 13, "God and Evil," which I wrote.

Van Inwagen, Peter. *Metaphysics*. 2nd ed. Boulder: Westview, 2002.

This book is a great place to begin to look at issues about free will and the argument about fine-tuning as well as other interesting issues such as the nature of persons. My diagrams in chapter twenty are adapted from some diagrams that van Inwagen uses in his book.

Hare, John. *Why Bother Being Good? The Place of God in the Moral Life*. Downers Grove, Ill.: InterVarsity Press, 2002.

This book covers a lot of ground about the relation between moral reality and God. It discusses the role of reason, community and the call of God in grounding the authority of moral claims.

Ganssle, Gregory E., ed. *God and Time: Four Views*. Downers Grove, Ill.: InterVarsity Press, 2001.

I edited this and wrote the introduction. The book presents four different ways to think about God's relation to time. Each author responds to the other authors' chapters.

Ganssle, Gregory E., and David Woodruff, eds. *God and Time: Essays on the Divine Nature*. New York: Oxford University Press, 2002.

I edited this book with my friend, David Woodruff. It contains a dozen essays that cover many of the issues concerning the nature of time, knowledge and God. It tends to be pretty technical, so it ought to be left for last of all the books on this list.

Beilby, James, and Paul Eddy, eds. *Divine Foreknowledge and Human Freedom: Four Views*. Downers Grove, Ill.: InterVarsity Press, 2001.

This book lists four of the major views about God's knowledge of the future. The writers interact with the views of the others in the book, so the reader gets a good picture of the strengths and weaknesses of each position.

Index